The Life of an American Holocaust Survivor:

Memories of the German Concentration Camps

By
Dana Kent

PublishAmerica
Baltimore

ISBN: 1-4137-9171-9
PUBLISHED BY PUBLISHAMERICA, LLLP
www.publishamerica.com
Baltimore

Printed in the United States of America

DEDICATION

This book is dedicated to my father, Mitchell Pawlak. I am thankful for his guidance and his unfailing memory in writing this book about his life. His helpful journal entries and information about his remarkable experiences made this book possible. He painstakingly provided me with all his thoughts, memories, photographs, and insights as I wrote this book, and for that assistance I am eternally grateful.

ACKNOWLEDGMENTS

Thank you to all the people who helped me put together this true story about the memoirs of my father's life and his experiences in the German Concentration Camps.

I thank my father, Mitchell Pawlak, for the many hours he spent writing journal entries about his experiences. I appreciated our long visits and conversations about his life and especially his experiences in the camps.

I thank my husband, David, for reading my story and giving me constant encouragement. His helpful computer know-how and technical ability made it possible to restore the pictures from my father's photo album so they could be included in this book. I sincerely appreciate all his help and unfailing support throughout this endeavor.

I thank my daughter, Cheryl, for helping with early organization and proofreading my initial efforts. She provided many helpful suggestions and ideas that helped make this book a reality. Her continual support is very much appreciated.

And I thank my daughter, Julie, for her encouragement when I was struggling with writer's block and needed a sounding board for some of my ideas. Julie helped me by reading my book and offering helpful suggestions.

FOREWORD

While I was growing up I often heard about the atrocities in the death camps and how many people had suffered unthinkable physical and mental tortures on a daily basis. Words like torture, brutality, death, horrible beatings, and agony were commonplace in my home as I listened to my father recount his experiences in the German concentration camps. He spent years incarcerated in those camps; he lost several years of his youth.

He would wake up at night in a cold sweat and trembling as he remembered those days vividly. Often he would tell us stories about how he had managed to escape death just by a moment. Or tears would come to his eyes as he remembered the lives that were lost in those camps. The people who died had lived in the hope that freedom would someday be theirs and they would somehow survive their captivity.

My father had memories of watching men, women, and children murdered in cold blood by the German soldiers. Age made no difference, the young and the old were treated alike. It was horrifying to hear how the German guards had shown little regard for human life as they slaughtered the innocent prisoners who became victims for no apparent reason. He told heart-wrenching stories of having witnessed the bravery of people he had come to know and respect. A few of them stepped in for other prisoners, to die in their place. He told stories about the living nightmare of that time period in history.

And I would listen in sadness, picturing the horror he must have witnessed time and time again. He had prayed for deliverance and freedom, but as the days became weeks and the weeks stretched into long, suffering months, he tried not to think of the future. When at last he was liberated, he was left only with memories of those dreadful camps.

Someday, I thought, the story of his life and experiences would have to be told. People should be able to learn about the American youth who was sent to the concentration camps because he was an American and a Catholic. This book is being written so people will learn more about the sufferings of human beings at the hands of other human beings. His story is the true story of one man who will never forget.

1

The Story Unfolds

Mitchell Pawlak became a survivor of one of the worst periods of history. He managed to survive countless tortures, beatings, and close encounters with death. After the war he wondered if a guardian angel had been sent to watch over him, to help him survive the atrocities and murders in the prisons and concentration camps of Germany and other parts of Europe.

He was left with terrible memories of the horrors he had witnessed, memories that have never left him and return frequently to haunt him. Deep in his heart is the belief that he had been blessed with many miracles. How else could you explain his ability to stay alive for more than three long and desperate years when people all around him were being murdered on a daily basis?

He spent three unbelievable years in concentration camps. Long periods during that time were spent at Concentration Camp Dachau, known to be a death camp from which there was no escape. Over the course of those years he felt many emotions. He felt frustration at being detained without any hope of escape. He felt fear that death would be his only relief. He felt sadness that he couldn't help the victims he was forced to watch being murdered without provocation. He felt despair at the hopelessness of his situation. He became depressed many times when he watched other men killing themselves rather than facing the inevitable. And he felt disbelief that human beings could treat other human beings in such a terrible way.

After the war, when he had finally been liberated from the concentration camp, Mitchell was left with a lot of memories. He could remember watching men being beaten and flogged. He had listened to their screams of terror, knowing there was nothing he could do to help them. He had memories of his own tortures, beatings, floggings, and the prison life that seemed to have no end. His life has been filled with agonizing pain and heart-wrenching frustration.

His courage in the face of death and his deep faith in God had managed to see him through situations that would have left him a statistic in history. Somehow he had survived the hunger, thirst, agonizing pain that was too readily inflicted, and tortures that were routinely meted out by men who enjoyed seeing their victims writhing in pain and suffering. He had managed to survive bombings, machine gun firings, clubbing that had killed weaker individuals, sickness, and countless other events. But he had a will to live that was strong, and he had a belief that he would somehow live to see another day.

Let Mitchell tell you the story of his life himself and how he became a survivor of one of the worst periods of history. Mitchell Pawlak is my father, and he was a survivor.

2

Memories of the Past

It was Christmas day, and my entire family had gathered together to enjoy the holiday together. It was dinnertime, and we were all sitting around a long table feeling the warmth of a traditional holiday get-together. I looked around at the faces that were full of anticipation for the meal we were about to enjoy. There was a large turkey, stuffing, candied yams, cranberry sauce, whipped potatoes, a large salad bowl, and all sorts of relishes. In the air there was a delicate aroma of a freshly-baked pumpkin pie, cooling in the next room for our dessert. Hot rolls and butter were brought to the table just as we began our blessing for the meal in unison. The gathering was at my daughter's home, and it was wonderful seeing everyone joined together in celebration.

My children and their families were present. It gave me a warm feeling to see my grandchildren sitting there also. There was a feeling of wonder that time had flown so quickly and I had grown-up grandchildren. As I looked around the room, I felt peace and contentment that we were all together on the holiday. But as the turkey was being passed around the table, I could feel a rush of tears come to my eyes as a sudden picture entered my mind and stirred memories of the past.

Instead of the beautiful scene in front of me, I had a brief recollection of a Christmas years ago that wasn't so pleasant. It was a meal that flashed into my mind just briefly. That Christmas I was alone, away from my family. I had been a young teenager who had been torn away from everything I loved simply because I was an American and a Catholic.

On that holiday, the German S.S. Guards had reminded the prisoners in the camp that it was Christmas. Then they had served our meager camp ration for us to feast on. It was a small slice of black bread, and a small bowl of watered-down cabbage soup. The vision flashed in my memory and then I pushed it away as quickly as it had come. This was a family gathering, and I didn't want haunting memories to take over our joyous celebration.

Pushing back the flash of memories was difficult, but I smiled pleasantly and took the platter of candied yams that had just been passed to me. It's funny how memories can sometimes come flooding in at the oddest times.

My name is Mitchell Pawlak and what follows are the haunting memories of my life and how I became a survivor of several years in the death camps.

3

In the Beginning...

I was born on the 22nd day of July, 1920, in Bayonne, New Jersey. My early childhood was nothing out of the ordinary. I attended elementary school in New Jersey until the 1930s. I had parents who cared for me, two brothers and a sister. I made friends easily in school and enjoyed playing with friends in my neighborhood, just like any other child.

But then in the early 1930s the depression came on with a vengeance. That event took its toll on everyone in the country and life became much more difficult. My father tried to keep our family life the same, but money was becoming scarce and it soon became a real struggle to make ends meet. It wasn't long afterwards that my father learned about a big farm that was available in Poland that he could afford. My family quickly packed up our belongings and made the life-changing journey to Poland to begin a different lifestyle. It was very hard to accept the move because I was leaving the teenage friends I had made and the life I had known.

We made our home in Mijakowo, which is in the county of Plock, Poland. My parents were able to provide a comfortable home life for our family on the large farm that was near the town. We always had food on the table, and I felt as if things were looking up. I was a young teenage boy who made close friends with other teenagers in the neighborhood, and very soon I was going to dances and other social events. There was always time allotted in my day to help my family take care of the farm.

We attended the Catholic Church known as "Swiecieniec" near Plock on a regular basis. My parents had raised me with a strong religious faith and a belief in the existence of God. I was an altar boy at our church, and I often helped serve the church whenever it was possible. When I was elected as president of the Catholic Youth Organization in my parish, it was a thrilling and eventful moment for me. What I didn't realize at the time, though, was that the event also marked the beginning of a fateful journey in life over which I would have no control.

Suddenly world events went out of control and nothing remained the same. In September of 1939 war broke out between Poland and Germany. When Poland was taken over by Germany, my younger brother Casimir and I decided that we had to return to America. My older brother had already enlisted in the armed forces because he wanted to get involved.

We began corresponding with the U.S. Embassy in Berlin, trying to arrange for our return to America. It was like hitting our heads against a brick wall. Red tape made it seem almost impossible, but we continued requesting assistance from the embassy officials to help us in our quest.

Workers at the Embassy informed me that my brother and I would have to arrive at the Embassy in Berlin to make the necessary arrangements. Twice we traveled to the Embassy, on the 10th of December, 1940, and again on the 10th of May, 1941. To be able to travel to Berlin, we had to obtain a pass from the German Police, known as the Gestapo. This we were able to accomplish easily and made the trip both times, hoping for assistance in getting back to

America.

At the embassy, while they were arranging for our passports, they informed me that because of my age I would have to register with the Selective Service. My brother Casimir didn't have to register because he was two years younger than me. I learned that in America there was a new requirement for registration because President Franklin D. Roosevelt had signed the first peacetime draft law on September 16, 1940.

I would have to register, take the oath of allegiance to the United States, and sign my name over my picture across my forehead because that signified that I had taken the oath. My younger brother signed his name below his picture, which meant that he had not registered or taken the oath of allegiance. This new requirement created a number of problems, as I was soon to discover.

It was around this time that one of our neighbors wanted information about obtaining papers for their children. The family lived near our farm and had a daughter my age. That was how I met Jean, my future wife-to-be. She was twenty years of age and had a younger brother, Eddie. But there was little time for courtship because the war broke out between the United States and Germany. We were not able to leave for America as we had planned. Everything had changed in a matter of days and our lives had changed drastically for the worse. It became dangerous to be an American living in Poland.

The Gestapo began immediately arresting Americans. I learned that Eddie, Jean's fifteen-year-old brother that I had just met, had been dragged out of bed at ten o'clock in the evening, and he had been taken to prison where he was badly mistreated. He was sent to a hard labor camp, and later he was transported to an American Internee's Camp in Laufen and then to Titomunic, Germany.

Not long after that I was stopped by the Gestapo, and they asked me for my identification papers. They discovered that I had taken the oath of allegiance to America from the picture with my name signed over my forehead, and they called me an "American spy." Though they were suspicious about me, I was released for the time being.

My family feared even more for the safety of Casimir and myself. My older brother Zigmund was in the service already, He had enlisted in the Polish army. Everyone in the neighborhood was talking about how Americans were being arrested without provocation and badly mistreated and tortured. My parents became really frightened for our safety and urged us to go into hiding. They were afraid that if the German Gestapo learned we were Americans, we would be taken away and killed.

My father had arranged a unique hiding place in a huge barn that was on our farm. The barn was set just a short distance from our home. My brother and I were hidden in pig stalls that were then covered with wood planks and lots of straw. The space was tiny, but it gave us enough cover when hiding became necessary. We hid there a few days later when it was learned the German police knew we were in the vicinity. When the Gestapo came to arrest us, they were unable to find our hiding place.

The hiding place worked for a few days, but it became evident that we would have to leave the area because the safety of our family was also in jeopardy. It was a struggle to live under these circumstances; we couldn't leave the house or even venture out into the town for fear of being discovered. Plans were soon arranged for us to disappear from the area by traveling to the large city of Warsaw.

We had learned that some of the counties around Warsaw were being allowed to be run by the Poles. The Germans retained rule over them, but they were operated by the Polish people. It was called "Protectorate," and they remained in German occupation. The areas had border lines around them that were patrolled by German guards. We knew that it was very difficult and dangerous to attempt to pass through the border, but we decided there was no other alternative.

At the same time we discovered that there were people who would help anyone who wanted to escape, if they could afford to pay their fee. They were willing to assist with the arrangements and we contacted them immediately. The only drawback was that they would only be able to take us part of the way across to our destination. We talked over the options we had with my parents, and finally decided to make an attempt to flee.

We had to wait until they had between six and eight people ready to make the journey. The few days we waited were filled with anxiety and tension. The actual travel didn't frighten me because I knew that the trip itself was only about one hundred kilometers, which is about sixty miles. We continued to hide on our parents' farm while we waited for word that our turn had come. And it didn't take long.

It was finally arranged for Casimir and me to make the journey on the 9th of December, 1941. We were escorted at night to an unknown location where the group came to a stop and issued special instructions. The people in charge said that the closer we came to the border, it would be important that no sound be made and that there was danger of being seen. We would all have to "walk like geese" to avoid detection. We were to go single-file, waiting until the person ahead of us was about fifty feet away before me moved forward.

One of the men in our group was very near-sighted, and he had trouble seeing more than a few feet in front of him. The impending darkness that created a cover for us also made it extremely difficult for him to see. He happened to be the second person in line. As he was walking behind the person in front of him, he mistook a tree for the person he was following; and we all followed him until we realized that we were lost in the swamps. We were in serious trouble because we couldn't tell how close we were to the border.

It was a rough night, but we somehow managed to get across the border. Our group reached a train station that was nearby; but we couldn't go inside the station because we could see several Gestapo watching closely. The trains were usually overcrowded, and there was a lot of activity in the area. From where I was huddled, I could see a lot of people milling about.

We waited in the field nearby until we saw the train come into view. When it had stopped completely, we ran to the side of one of the cars and managed to climb on top of the roof. There we laid down flat and held on while it picked up speed and traveled to the eastside Warsaw train station.

The ride seemed to take forever, though in reality it was only a short time before we arrived at our destination. As the train pulled into the station, we saw that the area was crowded with people. There were a lot of Gestapo walking around, I saw a sea of German uniforms with guns at their side. It was frightening to realize they were all around us.

When the Gestapo moved toward another part of the station, it appeared that we had a few minutes to make our move. We all climbed down carefully and began walking toward the tunnel that led to the street. One of the Gestapo turned at that moment and saw me standing nervously near the train. He became suspicious and I was stopped on the spot. He immediately placed me under arrest, pulling out his revolver and aiming it at me as he shouted for me to halt.

In a panic, I looked around to see if there was anything I could do in the situation. I could see that we were standing near a stairway that led to the tunnel. And we were near a small fence that led to the stairway. I could also see that there were three other Gestapo officers directly in front of me.

My thoughts raced through my mind as I tried to figure out a plan of action. I was certain that this would be the end of me if I didn't do something to try to escape. Without further thought, I shoved the three German officers to the ground in the direction of the train and threw my luggage down the steps. As quickly as I could manage, I jumped down to the tunnel steps and began running for my life. I could feel my heart racing, and I was gasping for breath as I ran for my life.

Running through the tunnel, I could see that people had to stand in line to pass through a small gate where another Gestapo officer was standing guard. When I jumped down, I had somehow managed to grab my luggage and started to walk at a rapid pace toward that gate. There was a long line, but I ignored the people and just walked as quickly as I could to the front. Luckily, another man from my initial group was about the sixth person in line and he could see me coming. He stopped and made enough room for me to get in line just in front of him.

We just managed to pass through the gate as the Gestapo officials began stopping everyone in line. By now night had fallen and the cloak of darkness engulfed the entire area as we ran out from the station and crossed the street. There was some type of construction going on, and I noticed a high barbed-wire fence around the entire construction area. We managed to run just past where the fence came to an end and found some low sunken areas. There we laid down quickly, lying as flat as we could, in an effort to avoid being captured.

As the Gestapo officials came out of the station, they were already shooting in our general direction, but they stopped when they reached the barbed-wire fence. They stood there for what seemed a long period of time. I held my breath, wondering if they would look in our direction and see our shadows in the darkness. Finally, though, they abandoned their search, and we watched as they left the area.

We stayed hidden for a long period of time before we felt it was safe enough for us to return to the station area. I searched every face among the crowd until I was able to find my brother Casimir. Together we crept forward carefully to avoid suspicion, walking away from the station and out into the fields of the town. We kept walking for a long time, not knowing if we would be discovered by the wrong people or finally find a safe haven. It was frightening, not knowing what would happen next.

As we continued our journey, I glimpsed a house that was nearby. We were happily surprised to meet up with another man who had been in our group. He was shocked to see that I had made it. He claimed that it must have been a miracle that I hadn't been shot. He had seen the Gestapo officers stop me and couldn't believe I had managed to escape their clutches. After talking briefly, we decided that it would be best if we parted and traveled separately in different directions.

My brother Casimir and I continued walking along, trying not to arouse suspicion, until we reached the main part of Warsaw. At length we reached the home of one of our cousins. We discovered that he owned an Auto Shop in the city with another partner who was a friend of his. He was willing to help us hide out for a while. He contacted another cousin in the area, and by the next day they were able to provide both Casimir and myself with fake ID's that had our pictures on them and with fake birth certificates for our new identities.

We were given jobs at the Auto Shop so people wouldn't suspect who we were. Both my brother and I were given different names, and we worked as mechanics for the next several weeks. Though I had only a limited knowledge about auto mechanics, I was made a supervisor in one section of the shop.

Though the work was strenuous and I had very little experience with working on cars, I found that I was able to perform the work satisfactorily enough to continue the pretense. I learned quickly and understood the mechanics of the job. That made the other workers respect me and accept my supervision without question. Casimir worked for about two months, but he became frustrated with the working environment and wanted to return home. Arrangements were made for him to go back to the home of my parents.

Luckily, he didn't get stopped by the Gestapo. Once he returned to our farm, my parents were able to obtain German identification papers from a family they knew that lived in the area. The family had recently lost one of their sons, and they provided him with their son's papers so Casimir could walk about freely.

4

Discovery and Arrest

In April of 1942 I learned that my mother was very sick, so I decided to return home to visit her. I made arrangements to return to the farm and left early in the morning on the 24th of April. As I was close to home, a Gestapo Officer appeared from out of nowhere on a bike. I had been walking along the side of the road, trying to watch the area to avoid being seen. But he had rounded the bend before I could find a place to hide. He recognized me at once from a previous encounter and came straight towards me. My worst fear was realized as he said that they were looking for me and that I was under arrest.

It was a known fact that anyone arrested by the Gestapo ended up being sent to the concentration camps. The Gestapo had no respect for the law, they disregarded all existing laws. I knew that those individuals unlucky enough to get arrested would be mishandled and sent off. The camps were used to eliminate opposition of any form, and they were regarded with terror by everyone. In my case, the German police wanted me because I was an American and a Catholic youth leader so they falsified my identity in their records for their own convenience.

It was about three miles to the police station, and he prodded me to begin the long walk to the Gestapo headquarters. He walked with his bike alongside as he led me to the station. Just then a young woman happened to be passing by on a wagon being pulled by a horse. The Gestapo Officer gestured to her to pull over and stop. He requested that she give me a ride to the police station.

People didn't have much choice when they were stopped by the Gestapo, so she readily agreed. He stayed right by the side of the wagon where I sat, hanging onto it to prevent any chance of escape. I recognized the young woman immediately and knew that she lived in the village next to mine. I also realized that she knew my family.

At about the same time came the realization that I had my fake identification papers on me and that I needed to somehow get rid of them or I would be in even more trouble. As I was sitting on the wagon, I kept my arms crossed in front of me, and I carefully thought about a plan to hide the papers so they weren't visible. As we moved slowly towards the police headquarters, the Gestapo Officer would occasionally look off into the distance as he felt more secure that I couldn't get away. I watched him closely and when I noticed that he was looking in another direction, I very slowly managed to pull the fake papers from my breast pocket. As quietly as I could, I dropped them into the pile of straw where I was sitting and covered them over so they wouldn't be visible when I got off the wagon.

Once we arrived at the station, the woman was sent home. I was taken inside the station for interrogation. They searched me completely, but they found only my German papers that showed that I was an American. They questioned me for what seemed a long time, repeating the same questions again and again. They asked me where I was returning from. I replied that I had gone to visit my sister Jenny's home because she lived in the area. When they asked me where my brother Casimir was, I replied, "He must be at home. I haven't seen him recently."

At first they didn't believe me. They kept repeating their

questions, trying to confuse me to see if I gave different answers. But I stuck to my answers and tried not to say anything that could get my family in trouble.

When they realized I was not helping them, I heard them issue an order to travel to my home and to watch for my brother. A long time afterwards I learned that they had hidden in the lilac bushes around my house to lie in wait for him. Casimir had just been returning home on his bike, and that was when they came out of hiding. They quickly stopped him and told him he was under arrest.

My mother was inside the house at the time, but she heard the commotion outside and ran to see what was happening. She watched as Casimir dropped his fake ID papers in an effort to hide them, and she rushed forward to try to pick them up. Before she could reach them, though, the Gestapo officers had picked them up and realized what they were. He was in trouble.

They arrested him immediately and brought him to the station where I was being held. We were both interrogated repeatedly; the officers were rough and treated us harshly. They beat me with a club until I thought my bones would break, and they kept kicking both of us over and over again. My back felt bruised, and it hurt terribly as they pounded all over my backside in anger. I was sure my entire body must be black and blue because every muscle and bone felt like it was on fire. The pain was excruciating and I prayed silently that it would soon come to an end.

They put Casimir in the same cell with me, but there was little comfort from having my brother detained in the brutal captivity. He looked for any possible escape from the cell and saw a chimney where the bricks were loosened. He thought we could escape while the officers were away if we pulled out the bricks and went out the chimney area. But I shook my head. "No," I said. "What do you think would happen to our family and our friends if we escape? They would go after them and harm them."

He finally agreed that escape was not an option. I thought about his plan again silently, wishing there was some way out of this situation. But it seemed hopeless, and I felt we should wait to see what hand fate would deal us.

I was frightened because I didn't know what would happen next. My only thought during the brutal beatings that I endured was to try to stay conscious and mentally alert. My only goal was to stay alive. I wondered, though, if we would be allowed to live another day.

5

Detainment in German Prisons

The next day the Gestapo took me in a car and transferred me to the main prison in Plock/Schrottersburg where I was interrogated several times. When the officials dragged me into the interrogation room, they kept beating and kicking me many times. They accused me of being an American spy—sometimes they would call me the "American dog." I didn't know at the time what had happened to my brother, if he had been able to survive the brutal treatment. I could only hope and pray that he had somehow managed to stay alive.

It wasn't until a long time afterwards that I learned that Casimir had survived the interrogation. He had been taken to an Internment camp especially for Americans in Titomonic and Laufen in Bavaria, Germany. I was kept at the Gestapo Headquarters near the prison for more than three months. When I was fed, the meals were scant and barely enough to keep me alive. The German guards would bring me a slice of black bread that was coarse and dry, and I would receive a little water.

Several times a day they would ask me questions and then beat me when they didn't like my answers. Sometimes they would torture me so terribly that I thought I was going to die. They struck my head countless times with clubs until I could feel the blood from the bruises mixing in with my hair. My bloodied hair became a red cap on my head as the tortures continued.

With each visit, the Gestapo would discover new and more painful tortures to inflict. When I could hear them coming, my body would tense with dread and trepidation because I didn't know what to expect. On occasion they would beat me with a special type of whip that had metal ends. The whip caused a scar on the left side of my forehead that I still have today as a physical reminder of that horrible experience. The beatings also caused me to become partially deaf in my left ear.

My back was black and blue, and the pain continued to be excruciating. I was often punched in my stomach as if they wanted to punch a hole right through me, and it would hurt terribly. After the interrogation session, they would then leave me standing in the tiny room, facing the wall, for long periods of time.

One time I remember vividly, I was standing in the corner of their room and facing the wall when a Gestapo officer entered again and told me to turn around and face him. He called me an "American dog" and kicked me in the stomach so hard that I fell to the ground and was gasping from pain. I was frightened, thinking that they had ruptured my stomach. I thought the end had come and that I would not survive the assault. They accused me of being a Catholic underground leader because I was the president of the Catholic Youth Organization in my village. They claimed that I must be an American spy and kept on with their torture.

Over the next several weeks I was interrogated often and then beaten, kicked, and tortured cruelly and inhumanely. My body became swollen from the beatings, and the pain was almost more than I could endure. Name-calling was a daily occurrence as the accusations and threats to my life continued by the tormentors.

Even today I still have many scars on my body as a constant

reminder of those beatings. Mentally I struggle with the horrible memories and often suffer from severe headaches. My thoughts continue to drift back to that time of my life, and I struggle with the terrible memories of how they treated me.

On the 23rd of July, 1942, they decided it was time to move me again. I was transferred to a prison in Dzialduw in northern Poland, not far from Schrottersburg. My prison experience was similar to the other prison, the officials continued to hold me in a tiny room where they would interrogate me repeatedly. They would beat me many times, repeating their accusation that I was an American spy. Then I was thrown into a tiny cell to wait for the next leg of my journey, and I didn't know from day to day what would happen next.

6

Prison Transfer,
From Bad to Worse

On the 26th of July, 1942 I was transferred to another prison at Konigsberg in Prussia, Germany. This was near Lithuania and Estonia at the northeast border of East Prussia. At this prison the horrible beatings and frequent interrogations continued. They kept me in a tiny cell that was only six by nine feet for nine days, which felt more like nine months. The cell had no windows. It was barely enough space for anyone to move around and there was a terrifying feeling of being held captive without any chance of escape. It was obvious the Gestapo wanted the prisoners to feel helpless.

I was held there with fifteen other prisoners, and there was no ventilation. That made it extremely difficult to breathe as the air became stuffy, I didn't think we would be able to stay alive. I couldn't believe the horrible conditions we were forced to remain in, and I asked God, how could people do this to other people?

In the morning a shrill whistle was blown loudly throughout the entire prison area. The sound was ear-piercing. When I first heard the loud noise, my body jerked in sharp disbelief that such a sound could shatter the silence and cause so much pain to my ears. I came to hate the sound of that whistle because it signified the start of a new day. All the prisoners in the cell were ushered into the corridor. There was a flurry of activity as everyone rushed to find a place in the corridor to receive the meager meal they brought.

Each prisoner was given a cup of black coffee that tasted terrible and a small piece of brown stale bread. This was our breakfast. The coffee was not like the coffee I had enjoyed at home when it was fresh and prepared by my family, but the liquid was at least warm and filled the empty pit that was my stomach. And the bread was something solid, though you really had to use your imagination to make it digestible.

After quickly consuming the meager rations, we would stumble about dazedly, feeling frightened and confused from the cramped quarters we had just left. Everyone ate their breakfast quickly because no one knew when it would be taken away without warning. Survival became a real struggle, and I wondered how long we would be kept alive.

Our dinner was also meager, usually just a piece of bread in the beginning. Sometimes they would vary the menu slightly. About every third day, the German guards would give the prisoners the added luxury of a cup of soup for dinner, but it was often not digestible. They used potato peelings and rotten vegetables in watered-down proportions to prepare it. And as we ate, bugs would crawl all over our bodies. To eat the soup, the soldiers would line us up because they only had ten bowls available to feed us.

When a prisoner received a cup of soup, he knew that he had to eat quickly. He would have to use his fingers to lap up the soup if there was no spoon available. Once the guard reached the tenth person, the dish was automatically taken away from the first prisoners whether they were finished eating or not.

On the 2nd of August, 1942, they transferred me to another prison in Marrinburg that was in East Prussia, Germany. Over the next few days they continued to beat me at every opportunity. There were frequent interrogations that always had the same outcome. After being questioned, spat at and beaten, they would usher me back to the crowded little cell.

I discovered from the other prisoners who were detained with me that you couldn't trust anyone at this prison. They said that infiltrators had been planted in the prisoner group to try to learn information. As I looked about me at the faces of the other men in my group, I wondered who the infiltrator might be. But only frightened faces looked back at me, I think we all shared the feeling of despair and frustration.

On the 5th of August they moved me to a prison in Elbing, in East Prussia near Danzig. It was here that I learned that I was bound for Concentration Camp Stutthoff. I learned also that this was a terrible camp from which very few people were known to escape alive. My thoughts at this time were on why this had happened to me. Why was I being treated as a spy, and why did the Germans single me out as a threat? I realized that it was because the Embassy had classified me as an American with my signature over my forehead on my picture.

It was only much later that I discovered that the embassy officials could have sent me back to America back in May of 1941. When they investigated the possibility of my return to America, they learned that I didn't have the money to pay for my fare. They had in fact contacted relatives in the United States to obtain the needed money. My uncle in New Jersey was going to pay for the ticket, and the officials were waiting for the money to arrive. At the same time, according to normal embassy procedures, they had checked with the Gestapo officials to verify my identification as an American. That communication with the Gestapo had earmarked me as an American and ultimately led to my arrest.

Later I learned that no other American in Poland had been asked to register or take the oath of allegiance as I had. Other Americans had been arrested, but they were sent to the American Internment camps in Laufen or Titomonic in Bavaria, Germany. Some of them were later exchanged for Germans who were held in the internment camps in South America and in the United States.

7

My Guardian Angel?

My family was religious and had raised me as a devout Catholic with a strong belief in God. I have always believed that we have guardian angels watching over us, sometimes guiding us in our lives and helping to keep us safe. That thought was predominant in my mind quite often while I was in the camps. There had been many times when I expected death, only to be spared by what seemed to be a miracle each time.

Because of my deep faith and strong beliefs, I have always tried to do what was right and be honest in the way I lived my life. Sometimes that honesty got me in trouble with the other prisoners. I can especially remember an occasion when I was in the prison in Konigsberg. There were a lot of prisoners being transferred on a train to other prisons in Elbing, Marrinburg, and Stutthoff. The train at the station was a special train that had nine cells for the prisoners and a separate cell with a latrine.

While I was going to the latrine, a young boy who was only about sixteen years of age came into the cell. He asked me if I knew where he could buy some cigarettes. I replied that I had some in my cell so he handed me 20 German marks to get them for him. Knowing the train would be pulling out soon, I went immediately to my room and went to the man who kept cigarettes for us. But he didn't have any available right then, so I started back out the door towards the train to let the boy know. At that moment I saw the boy being taken off the train to go to another prison.

I ran up as quickly as I could manage and handed the boy his money. I apologized that there weren't any cigarettes and wished him luck and safety at the next prison. Some of my fellow prisoners were standing there as I returned the money and shook their heads in astonishment that I had returned the money instead of keeping it. But I knew in my heart that it was the right thing to do.

I headed back to our room, where the other prisoners were gathered and standing about talking with one another. When I came in, one of them said loudly, "Well, that boy is gone to another place, so we now have twenty marks for ourselves to spend."

"No," I answered quietly. "I gave the boy back his money. I managed to catch up with him at the very last minute as the S.S. Guards were leading him away. He was only a boy and he can make use of it where he goes next."

Some of the prisoners chastised me for being stupid. They said I shouldn't have returned the money, he wouldn't have been able to do anything about it once they were moving him to the next prison. But I knew in my heart that I had done the right thing. I felt my conscience was clear and that I had followed the right path. My only thought was that God would watch over the young boy in the new prison he would soon be in.

My life had been saved countless times when I had been certain that death was imminent. Surely God must have heard my prayers and protected me when I needed protection. I truly believe my guardian angel was watching over me and helped me stay alive until I finally managed to find freedom.

8

Arrival at Camp Stutthof

On the 6th of August, 1942, I arrived at Concentration Camp Stutthoff near Danzig, Germany. This camp was near the Baltic Sea and there were many swamps around the camp grounds. At this camp there was a registration process when they would ask for personal information before giving you clothes or an identification number. Everyone was given a prisoner number that was imprinted in large characters on the pajama-like outfit they were issued.

I remember the day well because it meant another change was taking place. The conditions at this camp were horrifying to imagine; it was feared by prisoners as being one of the worst concentration camps. I had heard stories about what went on in the camp from other people, though I had hoped they were only rumors. I was soon to discover the truth for myself.

As we entered the camp, the first street we came to was in terrible shape. The street was known as the *Lagerstrasse*, and it ran down the center of the prisoner compound. The pavement was painful to walk on. It was topped with crushed brick and lots of gravel. We all had to take off our shoes and socks to enter the gate, and that made walking along the *Lagerstrasse* very difficult.

There were capos standing on both sides of the street to greet us and they had whips in their hands. The "capos" were the trusted prisoners, often German criminals, who were allowed to torture and beat other prisoners without mercy. This authority was bestowed upon them by top ranking officers of the camp. A slightly more esteemed, alternative position of authority was bestowed upon trusted prisoners that were not criminals. These individuals that managed to obtain respect from the guards were the "orderlies."

The capos beat us savagely as we entered the camp and tried to walk across the street. It was difficult not to stumble and fall as our group of prisoners moved slowly on the crushed brick. By the time we reached our destination, Barrack No. 5, my feet were bleeding badly, and I could barely walk.

We finally reached our first destination in the camp. We had all been taken to the bath-house where we had to undress and our heads were shorn to prepare us for the next step. Then we were all ushered into the showers and herded together for the "cleaning process." The water alternated between boiling hot and ice-cold for several minutes to prepare the prisoners for the registration process.

Driven naked into the yard, we were then taken to an area where tables had been set up so the German officials could take down our personal information. This was where we received our identification numbers that was to be our sole means of identification at this camp.

Next we received the clothes that were to be worn daily. The clothes I was given were uncomfortable because they didn't fit well. The outfit showed visible wear-and-tear—they had obviously been worn before. We learned later that these clothes were inherited from other previous prisoners who did not survive their incarceration.

Besides the pajama-like outfit that was thrown at me unceremoniously, I had also received underwear and a pair of wooden clogs. These clogs were our shoes. They were too small and my toes felt crunched inside when I placed them on my feet. No questions were asked about what size was needed because the guards didn't care. They just handed out a pair of clogs to each person in line and brusquely signaled everyone to keep the line moving.

I was fortunate to have received the wooden clogs. Sometimes less fortunate prisoners were not even provided these shoes because there wasn't enough to go around. Without the shoes, it was extremely difficult to walk about the *Lagerstrasse*. Their swollen feet only added to the other tortures inflicted in this hell.

My prisoner number was then stamped on a special piece of cloth that was to be sewn on the trousers and coat of my outfit. There were also special markings that were added to signify different prisoner categories. A triangle was sometimes added above the number for a variety of reasons.

The triangles were of different colors, depending on the so-called reasons for which the prisoners were being detained. Red triangles were seen most frequently, denoting the political prisoners. Green triangles were usually given to the criminal offenders. Violet triangles were for religious fanatics such as a Jehovah's Witness. Homosexuality was signified with pink triangles. Even antisocial tendencies were marked, by triangles that were black.

The Jews had to wear an additional yellow triangle, each combined with a colored triangle that formed a Star of David. When a prisoner tried to escape and was recaptured, his triangle became a blue one that labeled him as a person who had to be watched closely. The triangles would also contain the first letter of the name of the country (in German) from which the prisoners had come.

9

First Days at Camp Stutthof

The first days would always be the most crucial for every new person entering the concentration camp. It is impossible to get used to the idea that you are being locked up. Men, women, and children were thrown into a situation over which they had no control, without any explanation. There was no court available where you could protest that you were innocent until proven guilty. There was no visible official who would listen to the pleas of the victims or the cries for mercy.

The first few days in the camp were a learning process. Everyone learned about punishments and the commands that were issued at a moment's notice. To not obey a command for whatever reason meant being punished with kicks, slaps, or worse. Many of the prisoners did not speak German, and everyone in the camps quickly realized that learning to understand the German words being uttered was another requirement for survival. Within a short time prisoners had to learn the German commands that were issued for everything.

The S.S. guards gave orders only in German. They would expect immediate compliance whether the prisoner understood what was being said or not. To not obey a command meant punishment, either kicks, slaps, or even worse. Sometimes a prisoner was killed because he hadn't understood what was being asked of him.

I could feel the urgent craving for freedom. This was my youth, and it was being taken away without reason. It was here I discovered that my name was not important. I was simply a number.

10

My New German Vocabulary

I hadn't known German before my prison life began, but survival meant that I quickly had to learn the vocabulary that became a part of my new life in the concentration camps. Among the first words I learned were the following terms, though as time went on, I was able to pick up other words when it was necessary.

Appel: Roll Call
Appellplatz: Area where prisoners assembled on the campgrounds
Arbeitskommandos: Work Details
Block: The barrack building where prisoners lived in the camp
Blockelster: Staff member in charge of entire barrack
Blockfuhrer: S.S. ranking, leader of a particular section
Bock: Stocks used for punishment
Essen: Food
Hauptmann: German army ranking, similar to a U.S. army captain
Hauptsturmfuhrer: S.S. ranking, similar to a U.S. army captain

Hihlaygane: Lay down
Jourhaus: Guardhouse that controlled entry into the prison grounds
Kapo (Capo): Trusted prisoner, usually criminals placed in charge
Komandant: Person in charge
Komanderfurer: Officer in charge of shift
Kommando: Prisoner work squad
Lager: Prison compound within the concentration camp
Lagereltester: Camp leader
Lagerfuhrer: Official who was in charge of the prison compound
Lagerstrasse: Name of the street running down the center of the cam
Moorexpress: Horse cart pulled by prisoners on which corpses were carried to the crematorium
Oberscharfuhrer: S.S. ranking, similar to U.S. army lieutenant colonel
Obersturmfuhrer: S.S. ranking, similar to U.S. army lieutenant
Pfahl: Stake used for punishments
Plantage: A large experimental farm on the cam grounds
Reichsfuhrer-S.S.: Head of the S.S., position held by Heinrich Himmler
Revier: Hospital barrack in the compound
Schiesstand: Shooting stand
Schrecklich: A term that meant something horrible
Straf Commando: Hard labor post
Stube-elster: Staff member in charge of a prisoner room
Taagesrom: Room where meals were eaten
Wasser: Water

11

Helping Each Other

We helped each other in the camp. The prisoners made it a point to educate any newcomer to the meaning of the German words they needed to know. I had quickly learned enough German words to understand what the S.S. guards were saying. And it was evident that it was a matter of life and death that every prisoner should become acquainted with the language. In our barrack we struggled together to learn the terms and words that were frequently spoken to us.

Early in our confinement we learned the importance of prisoner numbers. It was easy to remember your number because it was printed in big characters on each piece of your clothing. Prisoners would be singled out for torture or punishment at that time for any number of reasons.

The numbers were actually a convenience for the German guards. The guards would stand off at a distance from where prisoners were working and watch them with binoculars. If the guards thought prisoners were working too slowly, they would write down their numbers without their knowledge. Sometimes they would write down the number of a prisoner who was resting or because he had needed to relieve himself. Sometimes the numbers would be written down because the prisoner had fallen down from his weakened condition. And sometimes the number would be written down for no reason at all. Perhaps a guard had just taken a dislike to a prisoner's face!

When the prisoners later returned to the camp, the guards would call out several numbers. Those prisoners whose numbers had been called then had to step forward to receive 25 whips or lashes. They had a bench in the courtyard that was used specifically for this cruel punishment. While they were whipping the selected prisoners, they forced the prisoner being whipped to keep count. Even worse yet, the count had to be in German, which made it even more difficult to keep track. If the prisoner missed a number or became confused, the guard would simply start the whipping over again.

I can still remember the roll call when I was singled out. My number was called aloud after we had returned from working out in the fields. The S.S. guard must have written my number down because he didn't believe I was working as hard as I could. It was a shock to hear my number uttered and I jerked in disbelief. Then I stepped forward feeling tremors go through my body because I realized what was about to happen.

With trepidation I walked up to the bench. I had to bend over the bench so I was lying half on it while my legs remained in back. They reminded me to count the lashes or they would have to start over each time. The pain as the whip struck my backside was excruciating and I could feel every strike as if it was cutting through my skin with deep gashes. The length of time the whipping lasted seemed almost insurmountable.

The pain of the lashes stayed with me for a long time afterwards because it took a long time for the wounds to heal. The physical wounds eventually disappeared with only slight scars remaining, but the mental anguish that I suffered remained with me forever.

12

The Barracks

The barracks were overcrowded, as was the taagesrom where we ate our meals. At night we had to leave our clothes and shoes folded neatly on a bench and then retire to the next room to sleep. Our beds were very simple bunks that were actually wood planks arranged like beds. The wood planks had rotten straw strewn over them and that comprised our mattresses. The sleeping conditions were not very comfortable, but when there is no alternative you learn to put up with whatever is available.

The straw took on a horrible odor after a while that made it unpleasant to smell and the other prisoners would talk about our "comfortable beds" with humor. You had to laugh at whatever you could those days because humor is a scarcity amongst death. Some of the beds would have less of an odor than others, and they would become a luxury that was coveted by everyone. When a prisoner had to go out at night to visit a latrine, he would sometimes return to find his place had been taken by another prisoner.

The bunk beds had three tiers so more prisoners could be crowded into the barrack than there was actually room for. I quickly learned that it was better to sleep on the top tier. I noticed that orderlies who visited the room at night would walk around and strike the feet of the prisoners with their big sticks. If you were on one of the lower bunks, you would end up with many bumps and bruises before the next morning.

There was just one bathroom for everyone in the barrack to use, but it was usually out of order. Because it was shared by more than four hundred people, it was difficult to keep it working properly. It was actually just a simple hut that had a horrible odor that you could smell from a distance.

We quickly learned the importance of not making sounds at night that might bring unwanted attention. When a prisoner coughed at night or made other sounds to bring attention to himself, he would be beaten by the orderlies or block captains. Sometimes the guards would choose to take the prisoner outside to the latrine. There they would put a water hose into his mouth and pour water down his throat until he drowned. His body was then thrown out by the barracks onto a pile of corpses. The guards were careful not to be wasteful. They made sure to save the clothes, which could be given to new owners.

I can remember seeing men in the barrack who were there one day and not there the next day. It was a constant reminder to everyone that life was very uncertain and death could occur at any moment.

13

Roll Call

Roll call, *appel* in German, was a routine ritual that was feared and dreaded by everyone. This is how my day usually began, in the early morning at 5 o'clock. Sometimes the guards would wake us even earlier when they felt like it. A shrill ear-piercing whistle signaled each morning to remind us that we were still alive. In the morning we were not given time to dress or swallow the pitiful cup of black coffee that was our breakfast. As we heard the whistle, we raced to the doors like madmen in order to avoid the blows from the guards.

Appel was not confined to morning time; it was scheduled at varying intervals throughout the day. *Appel* was also called at the noon hour, after work, before we retired to our bunks, if there was an escapee, or just to count the prisoners at varying times. Everyone had to be in line for the roll call. Even dead bodies of prisoners were dragged outside to be counted.

We knew from experience that if a prisoner was late, he would usually appear in the yard in bare feet with a bleeding head. Sometimes he would have broken hands, or he would show other signs of a beating. There was no excuse for being late for *appel*. The guards and capos used their sticks, clubs, and whips on the prisoners, keeping everyone in line with brutality and terror.

Because of the limited amount of space in the barrack, we had almost no room to keep our clothes, just somewhere near us. Often it was difficult to find your clothes quickly, and that would cause the orderlies to beat and hit you with their whips or sticks. The routine was always the same. We grew to expect the beatings by the guards and orderlies as a commonplace occurrence.

If someone was missing or the numbers the S.S. Guards expected didn't match their list, the entire camp had to stand at attention in the courtyard until the discrepancies in the numbers were solved. Weather made no difference. Sometimes we had to stand at attention in the pouring rain. Sometimes we stood still even though the sun was hot and beat down on us unmercifully. Even the freezing temperatures didn't deter the guards from the endless routine of *appel*.

14

Work Routines and Daily Life

Prisoners were divided into work details that were then dispatched to the camp grounds, workshops, warehouses, maintenance areas, and custodial areas. Some of the prisoners were sent to work at the large experimental farm on the camp grounds, the *Plantage*. Other prisoners were ordered to work at the regional factories and shops that produced small arms, S.S. uniforms, paper, porcelain, and other products.

While we went out on work detail or to the different jobs at the camp, we were watched by guards all the time. There were no private or quiet moments when you could reflect on your circumstances. You lived in the eye of public scrutiny every minute and felt eyes watching your every move.

Sometimes, for no apparent reason at all, the S.S. Guard would take your prisoner number and put you into a "straf kommando" (hard labor post) where you had to go early to carry the kettles filled with coffee to the barracks or do other chores for punishment. The work detail would continue under this watchful eye until around noon when the guards would usher the group back toward the camp and let us return to our barrack for the noon meal.

The barracks were built on a small hill, and sometimes on a whim the guards would make our entire group sit in front of the barracks facing uphill for long periods of time before they would let us proceed to the meal. This was a very difficult way to sit and caused leg cramps and other physical discomfort.

My work was scheduled for the "wald kommando" where I had to dig ditches or work in the swamps pulling out stumps. If someone tried to work slowly or became tired while digging, he was taken off to one side with a group of other prisoners. When we returned to the camp for lunch, the group of tired prisoners would be marched behind us and left standing near the kitchen.

At first we used to think they had been singled out for better food, but we soon discovered that was not the case. As we returned to work, we could hear the capo telling the group that they would not get any food because "those prisoners who didn't work would not eat." The prisoners were often so weak by that time that they became unable to work. They would then be taken on a wagon to be gassed until dead and their bodies were later cremated.

One time while we were out working in the ditches, a big storm came upon us suddenly. The sky became very dark, almost pitch-black, and the thunder rumbled all around us. The guards blew their whistles for the prisoners to get into formation to return to camp. When they counted us, they discovered that two prisoners were missing, so we were left standing there in the storm until the prisoners were caught. That took almost three hours, and we had to stand at attention throughout the entire storm. The rain poured down heavily and there was lightning and thunder all around us, but there we remained until the prisoners were found.

Once they were captured, the Guards beat them both so badly that they died. Their heads were actually split in half from the beating. The guards selected some of the prisoners to carry their bodies back to camp. These bodies were paraded in front of the camp so everyone would see what happened to the prisoners that tried to escape.

When we got back to camp they sent us to take a hot shower. Standing in the storm had weakened many of the prisoners, and many of them fainted in the shower. These unconscious prisoners were heaped on a wagon and thrown on the pile of corpses that awaited cremation.

On another occasion I remember our group being called to get into formation in the courtyard outside, not far from the gallows. There were eight ropes prepared for hanging people, so we thought we were all about to die. I was frightened. I knew already that a prisoner could become a victim at any time and there didn't have to be a reason. The guards chose six prisoners from another group and marched them to the gallows. They hung them right before our eyes. We don't know why they didn't select eight prisoners. Perhaps this was to maintain our fear that we still might be chosen for those last two ropes.

The drudgery and horror of our daily lives continued. My work was a struggle as I tried to keep up with the physical hardship of the tasks they asked us to complete. The loads we had to carry were extremely heavy, making our tasks very difficult. The guards forced everyone to work at the work sites for what seemed an eternity.

Some of the work consisted of being sent for twelve to fourteen hours to work in a stone quarry or a gravel pit. There we had to carry heavy planks while also carrying wielding picks and shovels. We would have to hoist fat, heavy trunks onto our backs and carry them just because we were ordered to do so.

A vivid memory I have is of working in the dirty and filthy swamps; it was a tiresome task that seemed to go on forever. Much of the work was being done to clear the area for buildings, but the monotony and routine was exhausting. We had to use heavy carts to carry the debris, and these carts were towed by a cable.

The wheels of the carts were then placed on rails for transport to another location. The rails were not properly aligned, which created another problem. This misalignment often caused the carts to be derailed as they moved up or down the rails. When this happened, the entire crew of prisoners was beaten unmercifully by the capo in charge. The capos were helping the S.S. Guards in their control of the prisoner work groups. They were assigned as chiefs on these work details, and they were known for their use of brutality. They carried huge whips and clubs with them all the time.

The time I was assigned to work as a bricklayer was a memory that remains with me too. My group had been assigned to prepare cement and lay bricks. My job was to work with the cement and lay the bricks in the proper sequence for a retaining wall. Another prisoner I had come to know was assigned to get the bricks for me from a nearby pile.

He was a hard worker and was helping me perform the task without complaint. He would walk over to the pile of bricks, pick up several of them, and carry them to where I worked setting them in place. We had been working at the task for a few hours when I noticed that he hadn't returned with the bricks I needed. I knew the pile was just beyond our site, so I couldn't understand why he wasn't returning.

Then I learned that when there were no more bricks in the pile he had been going to, he had needed to go to another pile of bricks that had been placed in a special area where prisoners were not allowed to step. As my friend stepped into the area and picked up a brick, an S.S. Guard had shot him in the head, killing him instantly. The S.S. Guard smiled happily at the death as I mourned the loss of the prisoner I had come to know. I was certain the guard knew why the prisoner had crossed the line, but that didn't make a difference.

Sometimes during our imprisonment at this camp, our work detail would be changed because they needed manpower for other requirements. My assignment in the transportation squad was a terrible experience. I was placed in a harness with other prisoners and we had to pull huge wagons to cart materials or food from one area of the camp to another. Though we did our best to pull the load, the S.S. Guards would whip us on our backs and legs to get us to move faster.

The capos who supplemented the guards delighted in using their clubs and whips to beat and torture the helpless men in the work details. They would smile with glee when they saw that they had caused physical pain and suffering. It was unbelievable that they could enjoy the punishments and tortures as if they were enjoying a sport or a game. If they didn't have clubs or whips handy, they would sometimes use their fists, shovels, a stick, or whatever else was handy. We came to dread the sight of the capos as much as the other German guards.

The loads we carried sometimes included a huge amount of cabbage heads. I can still remember trying to grab some of the cabbage leaves from the load when the S.S. Guards weren't looking. Those raw cabbage leaves provided a little extra nourishment for the prisoners when our stomachs were rumbling from hunger.

Unfortunately, eating the raw cabbage had its downside. Many of us came down with a bad case of diarrhea. We knew that if we had to go to the toilet while working, we would be severely beaten. Rather than going off to the side to relieve themselves, often the men would just let go right where they stood. You could see the mess it made down their legs and in their clothes.

Many of the prisoners eventually became so weak that their weight dropped drastically. Prisoners learned from the beginning that falling on the ground from weakness didn't help. Everyone knew you couldn't expect mercy or help from any source. I had seen a prisoner fall from extreme exhaustion, and the capo simply walked over to him and looked at him coldly. Then he finished him off by jumping on top of him until he was sure he was dead.

As a teenager I had been of normal weight. But now my weight had dropped considerably. I became a thin shell of my previous self and began to look like a skeleton of a person. My legs and feet would often swell up, causing pain that seemed unending. Yet I wanted to live, my struggle to survive still raged within me.

The clothing they gave us did not keep us warm enough in the cold temperatures. I had to use what paper I could find to stuff under my shirt to keep from freezing in the severe cold weather. I also used the paper to wrap around my feet to protect them from the elements.

I learned that the added insulation to my toes prevented frostbite.

I was beaten while I was out working and again as I returned and was walking back to the camp. Behind each group of prisoners there would be a truck that followed closely by. It was filled with bodies of the dead or those prisoners who were too sick or weak to walk. The entire barrage of prisoners was always surrounded by S.S. Guards with German shepherd dogs held on leashes to help keep the group moving as quickly as possible.

Later the other prisoners would be forced to pull the bodies from the truck and dump them on a pile near the crematorium. It didn't matter if the prisoner was dead or alive—the end result was the same. Sometimes when a truck was not available or the truck was overfilled, the prisoners were forced to carry the bodies back to the camp on their shoulders.

The added burden would sometimes become too difficult for some of the other prisoners who had also become weakened while out working. If they were unable to carry their burden, they were instantly shot or beaten to death as a way of remedying the situation.

15

Dead Body Quota

Sometime during the late summer months of 1942, we were assigned to work at a site where we had to dig deep pits with shovels. The S.S. Guards kept pushing everyone to work faster, faster. Though I was working as hard as I could, the capo still passed by me and struck me with a whip to show his displeasure with my speed. As he passed another prisoner who was working near me, he struck him with his whip handle and laughed as the struck victim lost his balance and fell down. He tried to get up, but he looked too weak and just lay right where he fell.

The capo just finished him off with his feet. He was wearing heavy boots and I watched sadly as he jumped on top of the man several times to make sure he was dead. In silence I said a mental prayer that his soul would now be able to find peace and the comfort that he hadn't been able to find on this earth.

His body was then thrown on the wagon that followed behind our work detail. We could see his body lying on top of about thirty to forty other bodies. Most of the bodies were obviously dead, though a few prisoners could be seen lying weakly and close to death.

Later as we returned to the main camp area, our detail passed through the gate with the wagon being pulled behind us. The S.S. Guard at the gate asked, "How many dead prisoners do you have?"

The capo by the wagon answered, "Forty dead ones."

The S.S. guard shook his head and urged, "You can't do better?"

The capo replied, "I'll try for fifty tomorrow."

16

Change in Lunch Routine

Late in August, 1942, the *Komandant* decided that the workers weren't getting the work done fast enough. An order was issued that too much time was being lost when the work detail returned to the camp to have lunch. There would now be a change in the lunch routine. It was decided that the cooks would bring the food to us where we were working out on the field. They believed that would enable us to get more work completed.

When the cooks came out with the food, the capos tried to keep the prisoners in their work line. They walked around the prisoners while the food was being passed out and struck them with their sticks and clubs to get them to eat faster. Eating in the field was especially difficult because not only did you have to avoid the blows of the capos, you had to eat quickly while still holding on to your shovel and other tools. It created a big mess that every prisoner came to dread.

While this new lunch routine was in effect, the quota of dead bodies increased. The wagons would take back about two hundred dead bodies each evening instead of the usual forty or fifty.

17

Punishments at Camp Stutthof

Punishments were so ingrained in our daily lives, that they *became* a way of life. Punishments in this camp were very severe. To prevent monotony, the guards would discover many new ways to make us suffer. Sometimes prisoners were made to squat for long periods of time and tormented continually. Sometimes insults were hurled at them, and they could only stand or squat quietly, knowing that they could not retort or the reprisals would be even greater. This torture was especially difficult when the sun was very hot and we would squat for a long time, feeling our legs go numb.

Some of the S.S. Guards would beat the prisoners with their clubs without provocation or forethought. The guards would simply single out a prisoner and beat or kick him brutally until they could see he was suffering. It almost seemed like a game to some of the guards as they would try to come up with new ways to inflict pain. Tortures occurred often, and they were always physically and mentally horrific.

When lashes were issued as punishment, it was usually twenty-five lashes on the buttocks. They used sticks or whips, depending on what they had handy. Simple lashing occurred frequently and often it was without provocation.

The punishment of flogging was greatly dreaded because it was excruciatingly painful. The prisoner was taken to a special whipping-block, like a specially constructed stool, that was there just for that purpose. The official number of twenty-five strokes was often increased by overzealous S.S. Guards. These guards would continue their flogging until they counted out seventy-five strokes. The terrified victim was responsible for this counting, which had to be in German, during the flogging. If the prisoner made a mistake during the counting, the flogging would begin anew.

The flogged prisoners were then carried to a spot in front of the block where they would lay until they were able to move on their own back to their barracks. The other prisoners would look on helplessly, unable to offer assistance or comfort. I found it heart-wrenching to witness pain and suffering that took place so close to my person, but I could not move, I could not offer comfort. It would do no good.

Some tortures occurred despite weather conditions. Other tortures used these conditions as part of the torture. The guards enjoyed sending prisoners out into the cold or freezing temperatures to stand and shiver needlessly. A man would be pushed outside with very little clothing on so he could feel the full effects of the temperature. The winters were always freezing, sometimes going as low as twenty degrees below zero. But a prisoner would be forced to stand outside in the light pajama-like outfit (sometimes without the top portion on) depending on the whim of the guard.

Sometimes we would be forced to stand outside during heavy rains until everyone was sopping wet. If the sun was extremely hot at noontime, they would make us stand in the courtyard because they knew it was the hottest part of the day. The guards would smile and even laugh as they saw the sweat pouring down our faces. When they allowed us to sit, we were forced to sit with our legs facing uphill because they knew it was uncomfortable.

Often a prisoner was punished by being sent running for half an hour or longer. He had to carry a forty-pound stone past a line of guards who took turns whipping the prisoner as he passed by. If he fell down while running, the guards would kick and strike him until he got up again. If he was unable to stand up because of his weakened condition, they would simply shoot him and throw his body in the pile for the crematorium.

Caning was a punishment that was frequently imposed. The guards would take a cane or a club and strike the prisoner all over his body for any reason they found. The cane would leave marks on the skin and cause excruciating pain for the victim. It seemed inhumane for the guards to take such pleasure in hurting people, but it was evident that they enjoyed the practice when they would smile happily as they struck the poor man who was cringing at each blow.

Some offenses would merit solitary confinement. But there didn't have to be an offense to suffer this punishment. Sometimes the guards just didn't like the way a man looked. They would single him out for no apparent reason for this torture. The prisoner would be placed in a dungeon that was in total darkness. It was built so small that the prisoner placed inside could neither lie down nor stand up straight. They would be shoved inside and given no food or water for the designated period of time.

The use of solitary confinement was also used for prisoners who were too weak to continue performing their tasks or work. You could see the vacant stare behind the eyes of men who no longer had hope of escape or rescue from the daily tortures. They would be tossed into the little dungeon and left there without food or water. There they would remain until they died.

Yet another common punishment was being led into a shower stall. The prisoner would be hung with his hands tied behind his back and suspended from the shower head. There he would hang for several hours until his arms were close to breaking off. While he was hanging there, guards would come in and hit him repeatedly to add to the torture.

This position—being hung with hands tied behind the back—was implemented in other locations. Sometimes the guards would lead prisoners to trees in full view of the camp area. They would tie their hands behind their backs and then string them up from hooks that were attached to the trees.

Sometimes a prisoner would be tied to a stake in the yard and his body was lifted just enough so he could barely touch the ground with the tips of his toes. There he would hang by his arms that were tied behind his back until the guards returned to take him down. This punishment would often last for several hours.

I can remember being forced to witness this scene many times. Every time I saw someone being punished in this way I felt frustrated and had a feeling of helplessness, that I couldn't help the person being punished. The guards would continue to approach him and keep striking the prisoner on the head and face while he would hang there for two or three hours.

We learned to expect ruthless discipline and corporal punishment for even the slightest infringement. If a prisoner was slow to move, he would be forced to stand at attention for hours. Sometimes those hours would stretch into days.

Random shootings sometimes occurred just because the guards felt that there were too many prisoners in their area. They would simply pull out their pistols and fire at helpless men as they tried to avoid the shots. If they happened to strike a prisoner in a foot or a hand, they would quickly run up and finish him off because they believed an injured man couldn't work. We all became used to the sight of dead bodies lying around in the camp.

18

Meals at the Camp

Meals in this camp were scarce and unappetizing. Sometimes they fed us cabbage, and this would continue for the entire month. Then they would switch our food to another vegetable, like carrots. That would be the main course for the next month. They alternated with rutabaga, spinach, sometimes turnips. When vegetables weren't available, they used potato peelings for our meal.

Starvation became our worst form of torture. Hunger dropsy really changed the appearance of every prisoner. At times it made us look strikingly fat. Our faces became swollen and they were always dirty and unkempt. Our skin took on the color of decaying flesh, making our hands and necks appear even darker and older before our time. Our eyes were extremely bloodshot, and often filled with pus that was caused by the malnutrition.

Without even looking, you knew that the faces of the prisoners were without expression and that their eyes had become lifeless and sunken. I remember noticing how our cheekbones stood out and our lips always felt cracked and dry. Our skin always looked ashen and very pale.

People who are starving have trouble walking or even moving about. When prisoners walked anywhere, they would shuffle along and their bodies seemed to droop. Breathing was labored and difficult. Reflexes became sluggish as time went on, and many of the prisoners lacked the mental and physical stamina to even stay alive. When we would talk together in the barrack, we would notice when a man was mentally exhausted or feeling depressed.

The general rule everyone followed was to eat everything that was available, and we knew it had to be eaten as quickly as possible. Whatever was put in front of us was consumed without question. The food was a miserable replica of what a meal should be. It became a quest to find an extra slice of bread just to supplement the meager diet. It didn't matter where the food came from....sometimes it was grabbed from another prisoner who was too weak to fight back or complain.

In the beginning, my breakfast consisted of a piece of black bread that was barely digestible and a cup of *ersatz* coffee or tea. Sometimes we were given only the liquid and even that was often undrinkable. The slight meal was eagerly anticipated, even though we knew it had to be rushed because we had to make roll call.

Our lunch was usually around noon, and we received about a liter of thin soup that was usually made from dry vegetables and potato peelings. I would sometimes reminisce about the meals at home. I would remember times when I would not want to eat something my mother had made. I realized now that I would eat anything put before me just because of my hunger.

Our supper was slightly better because they added a pint of very watered-down cabbage soup (or whatever vegetable was available that month). They would add whatever they could find to the soup as an ingredient. Rotten potatoes were a staple, though they liked to add turnips mashed in water or potato peels to the soup for variety. Our drinking water was often dirty and mixed with mud. Sometimes unpeeled potatoes were blended with mud. Whatever food they gave us was watered down so much that it was only slightly recognizable as food.

Earlier in my captivity at this concentration camp, some of the meals were varied with small slices of cheese, marmalade, or even *ersatz* honey on occasion. But as our length of stay continued, the food became scarcer and was left to the discretion of the camp guards. Sometimes the amount of food that was doled out to each person varied on the whim of the guard dispensing it.

The guards often gave us a thin slice of black bread that was very coarse and difficult to swallow. The piece was about one-eighth of a loaf of sour black bread that was a common staple in our diet. Even a few extra crumbs of bread would sometimes make the difference between life and death from starvation. For some of the meals they would bring a very small amount of poor-quality sausage. But when we had soup, the bread and sausage was eliminated.

The rations given to us had been calculated to keep a man alive for a maximum of three to six months. The food or lack of it often caused severe health problems for many of the prisoners. Stomachaches were common. Hunger caused a rumbling noise that could be heard when it was quiet. Men were dying all around me.

Prisoners sometimes tried to help each other when they noticed the men that they worked with had become very weak. It was difficult to give up your food to a weaker friend when your own stomach was rumbling with hunger pangs. Still, I saw many instances where men gave up their rations to a weaker man and later tried to find potato peelings in the garbage or take pieces of wood chips to chew on just to survive. Sometimes I had to eat charcoal from wood that had been burned for heating the tar for roofs just to survive. The conditions caused me to suffer from severe diarrhea.

Diarrhea is a common occurrence when you have long periods of starvation, and many of the prisoners suffered from this. With the few latrines available, that meant that sometimes a man would not be able to make it to the facility in time. If a guard noticed diarrhea running down a prisoner's legs and onto the floor, that prisoner's life was in danger.

Many of the prisoners in my barrack had a lifeless appearance that made them look much older than their actual years. Their eyes looked sunken and hollow. Their bodies looked like skeletons and their cheekbones were clearly visible. Many prisoners died from typhoid fever.

While we were out on work detail, we would search for muddy roots to eat because we were always starving. It could be leaves in the mud or pieces of wood that were on the side of the road. Sometimes prisoners would find earthworms in the swamps and greedily eat them so they could live. Anything we found became a necessity for life. I longed for a home-cooked meal or just any escape from the torture.

Everyone began searching for pieces of charcoal from the burned-out wood to eat because we had heard that charcoal was supposed to be good for our stomach disorders. We would eat any kind of rubbish in order to survive. As I looked around at my fellow prisoners, only grim and haggard faces looked back at me, their eyes often looked feverish as though desperately wishing for a sudden and merciful death to escape this captive life.

19

No End in Sight

As time went on, I found the conditions in my barrack even more difficult to survive. The bunks were still three-tiered, with very little space to lie down. We couldn't sit upright because the space was much too small. Our only covers were the filthy blankets they gave us. Though the bunks were originally intended for four people, the tiny beds usually had to hold ten or more occupants. As we gasped from the lack of air, the air we managed to breathe was heavy with foul odors.

Many of the prisoners never recovered from this inhumane treatment, they were discovered dying or dead in their bunks. The conditions were so horrible that some of the men in my barrack just gave up. They could see no end in sight and weren't able to cope with the desperation they faced daily.

Some of the prisoners would commit suicide by using the electrified wires that surrounded the camp. When they realized how hopeless their situation was, they would take whatever physical strength they had remaining to run into the wires. If the electric current didn't kill a man, he would be shot by the S.S. guards who guarded the prison areas.

20

My Experience with the Infirmary

Most concentration camps had an infirmary. The prisoners often thought of these infirmaries as "finishing chambers." The infirmaries did not have real doctors. These had not existed in the camps for a long time. When I talked with the other prisoners, I learned that some of the so-called "doctors" had actually been carpenters, painters, or other craftsmen before being assigned medical positions at the camp. Untrained prisoners (usually German criminals) were assigned the task of treating anyone who came in with a health problem.

Some of them even performed major operations, though they were ignorant of medical techniques and practices. Most of the time prisoners would die from their illness at the camp infirmary. Those prisoners who couldn't be helped would simply be disposed of in a gas chamber. It became common knowledge that it was important to avoid being sent to the infirmary whenever possible. It was easier to overlook the pain and suffering in order to avoid possible death.

Because my legs were having severe problems and my health was badly deteriorating, I was sent to the dreaded camp infirmary. When I arrived at the medical station, I was thrown into a chair until I could be seen. Fear and dread were my companions as I waited. Finally, a self-made doctor came into the room. He was German and very brusque in his manner. There were no questions asked about why I had come or how I was feeling, he just looked me over. Without hesitation he said they would have to operate on my foot immediately.

The operation, if you can call it that, is burned into my memory. He called two S.S. Guards over to hold me down tightly while he operated on my right foot. He took a big knife from the table and cut my foot open in three different places. Next he pushed the knife through my entire foot directly behind my toes, and he stepped back as if the task was complete. The entire operation had been performed on me without any anesthetic.

The pain was excruciating. I screamed in agony from the horror of what was being done to me. I was unable to suppress my feelings, and I felt certain that I was about to die. Just when I thought I couldn't take another moment of the pain, the S.S. Guards carried me to another room nearby. They threw me on a wooden slab and left me there, writhing in agony.

This was a room where prisoners were usually thrown to die in a pile while waiting for cremation. I was certain that I had been left there to die in lonely isolation. One of the camp orderlies who had gotten to know me over the past few weeks was passing by and he stopped. He told me that whoever comes into this room is scheduled for the pile of dead corpses.

I was shocked when he also said that he would try to get me out of the room as soon as he could. He left for a while, and I started to worry that he wouldn't return. I faced the realization that I would soon be another dead body on my way to the crematorium. But he came back hours later and moved me to another room where I was able to recover.

To this day I still have scars on my foot and my walking is

affected. Vivid memories of that terrible operation cause me to wake up screaming from nightmares as I remember that scene again and again. It's difficult to forget the pain and suffering I endured not only from the operation but while laying in that little room thinking death was near. The pain was excruciating but even worse was the realization that death was always near and waiting for its next victim.

21

The Transport

Late at night on the 9th of November, 1942, three S.S. Officers came into our small room and called for everyone to rise from bed. They ordered everyone to stand at attention and to hold our charts in front of us. We climbed sleepily from our bunks, not knowing what to expect and feeling very frightened. At that point three German officials entered, and they looked us over very carefully.

We were frightened, not knowing what would happen next. Slowly they walked among us and looked at each prisoner carefully. There were ten of us standing there, and they picked me out from the entire group. They ushered me from the barrack and took my identification card away with them. I was the only prisoner in the barrack who had a red triangle on my card. That symbol, of course, meant that I was political and dangerous for Germany.

I became even more frightened, not knowing what to expect. Before my arrest I had witnessed how Germans had often gathered Jewish men, women, and children and shoved them into trucks. I had heard how the trucks drove them out to open fields. It was rumored that guards would execute them near a deep hole that had been prepared in advance, for quick burial. I felt certain that this was about to become my fate now.

I was taken to a room where I discovered about five hundred other prisoners being held in confinement. We didn't know why we had been singled out so we waited together in that room. There we remained for the entire night. We each received a small piece of bread. At the time, we did not realize this would be our last meal for several days. It wasn't until late the following day that they herded us together outside and marched us along roads to a nearby train station.

We were loaded in cattle boxcars on one of the trains. Many of the prisoners were so weak that they couldn't climb into the boxcar themselves. I felt very weak and didn't know if I had the strength to keep going. My helplessness at the situation I was in added to my feeling of despair. The Gestapo ordered some of the other strong prisoners and some of the S.S. Guards to throw about forty of us into the car and close it tight.

There we sat for a long time. The train did not have a good connection, and it sat on the side waiting to be hooked up when the locomotive came. It was not scheduled for a long time and it was freezing cold outside. The boxcar had no warmth so we huddled closely together trying to stay warm.

There was no food or water. Hunger, thirst, and the cold soon created an air of impending doom. My stomach grumbled and I could hear the sounds of other stomachs complaining about the lack of food. But even worse was the feeling of thirst. I yearned for water. There was no water anywhere and we had no idea when or if it would ever be available. I tried to picture myself sometime in the future drinking lots of cold water that was soothing my parched throat. But reality would quickly dispel the dream, and I would moan with the other prisoners.

There was a small crack in the door of the boxcar that allowed a slight glimpse of the outside surroundings. On one occasion we could see someone passing by, and the prisoners began moaning and crying out for food. A man came up and said, "I would like to give you food, but the doors are locked with padlocks." He left as our cries filled the air and the tortured moans of the sick and weak men continued into the night.

On another occasion, an S.S. Guard came up to the boxcar. I held my breath for a moment, praying that he would let us out of our confinement. He pounded on the door until he heard a stir. His only questions were, "How many of you are dead?" and "How many of you are still alive?" He left then, and again we were waiting. Only we didn't know what we were waiting for.

The conditions became even more disgusting. The air became very stifled and suffocating. There were no latrines in the boxcar. The stench of urinal buckets that were standing in the corner of the cars was terrible. Prisoners went wherever they had to. The buckets had overflowed, creating a very foul odor that made it almost impossible to breathe. The smells of the dead corpses added to the horrible odor.

The journey was inhumane and it felt like a living nightmare. We were all crammed together like cattle with no food or water for the entire period that extended to over a week. We only knew that we were headed for Concentration Camp Dachau, and that would be our new home. We had no idea when we would arrive at our destination or if we ever would. If we reached our destination, we expected even more torture or possibly death.

Many of the prisoners never reached our destination. Everyone felt the pangs of hunger and became very weak. Everyone suffered from the bitter cold. Countless prisoners died because they were too weak to survive those conditions, and some of the remaining prisoners frantically began eating the carnage. The prisoners who didn't resort to cannibalism began chewing bits of wood chips they were able to tear off the boards in the boxcars.

Vivid memories of that experience remain with me constantly. Sometimes at night I wake up in a sweat believing I am still in that boxcar waiting with the other prisoners. It takes me several minutes to finally realize that I am actually home. I take a deep breath and say a prayer of relief that I am alive.

Once the transport arrived at Camp Dachau, many prisoners had to be carried off the boxcars because they were too weak to climb down themselves. It was difficult to stand because of the weakness and dizziness everyone felt. I took a deep breath of air in relief to finally leave our tiny confinement space. It was a sight beyond belief. And I remember the terrible thirst. I could feel my parched lips longing for a drink of water or anything liquid.

I can still remember getting off the boxcar and seeing all the dead bodies. There were lots of dead bodies. Many of the bodies were missing parts: ears, noses, and other parts of their faces. Sometimes the genitals of prisoners had been bitten off. Several of the bodies had the flesh of their buttocks eaten off. Even more mutilated corpses were discovered later in those same boxcars.

We arrived in Dachau on November 19, 1942. It was around eight o'clock in the evening. Though five hundred prisoners had been transferred originally, only about eighty of us actually reached the camp alive. The rest died. This had been one of the worst transports to arrive at Concentration Camp Dachau.

22

Concentration Camp Dachau

Camp Dachau had 36 barracks and the camp was divided by a wide street called by its German word, *Lagerstrasse*. On one side were all the even-numbered barracks, and on the other side they had the odd-numbered barracks. On the south side of the camp was the Appellplatz, the assembly place for prisoners. Along the fence that straddled the prison compound were the guard towers. In the center of the camp, amid a cluster of trees outside the northwestern corner of the prison was the camp's gas chamber and crematorium. Most of the buildings that were in the vicinity were workshops and laboratories that were run by slave labor. The buildings that housed the S.S. officers and guards who ran the camp were visible nearby, in the large courtyards not far from the prison street.

The two sides of the camp were separated by an eight-foot-high barbed-wire fence. Each barrack was built to accommodate 650 people, but more than nineteen hundred prisoners were forced to live in each building in crowded conditions. In the barracks there again were the three-tiered bunk beds like in the other camp that were actually meant to be shelves, not beds. When the camp hospital ran out of room for the sick or recently deceased prisoners, they were stored in the barracks.

Prisoners were not allowed to go out without a reason or without an escort. Many of the prisoners in this camp were used for experiments at the camp hospital, and officials would come into the barrack and select men to be taken out for research purposes. If there were too many men in the room, guards would come to the room at night and drag several prisoners at random to be carted off to the gas chambers.

Camp Dachau was the centerpiece of Himmler's police state. Reichsfuehrer Himmler was known to be Hitler's right-hand man. And he was the main inspector of all the concentration camps. The camp had opened on March 22, 1933 on the grounds of a former ammunition factory. It was created to house the undesirable elements that Adolf Hitler wanted out of the way. The Jewish people were the primary occupants, but they weren't alone on Hitler's list of undesirables. Political opponents and the clergy also became occupants in the camp. And the list kept growing at a very rapid pace.

Within four years the camp became too small to house the many prisoners being sent there. When it was originally erected, it was meant to hold 5,000 prisoners but it became evident as time went on that more space would be needed. The first oven was installed at Camp Dachau in 1939 to dispose of political prisoners, and at first it was able to cremate two corpses an hour. By the 1940s a single crematorium was burning more than a thousand corpses a day.

Prisoners were forced to build a new and larger camp, and that camp was completed in 1938. By 1945 the camp held more than 20,600 registered prisoners. There were countless other prisoners who were never even registered. There were more than two thousand Catholic priests. More than 31,000 prisoners met their deaths in the camp, while there were thousands more whose deaths were not even recorded.

This camp was not known as a death factory, the way Auschwitz was. The guards used other methods to kill people. Some prisoners were gassed, some were cremated. Shootings, hangings, clubbing, bayoneting and other methods quickly eliminated many prisoners. Sometimes prisoners were sprayed with ice-cold water until they froze to death. Savage dogs were sent in to rip prisoners apart. And sometimes prisoners were simply scheduled for extermination by being placed in the gas chambers.

Dachau was known to be a training site where the inhumane concentration camp system was perfected. The camp actually paved the way for the infamous practices of extermination camps as Camp Auschwitz, Camp Majdanek, Camp Treblinka, and others. A gas chamber was installed at Dachau and it was camouflaged as a huge shower room. There were four incinerators that made up the chamber. Extermination was affected by gassing, brutality, hunger deprivation, or simply illness.

23

Arrival at Camp Dachau

When we arrived in Camp Dachau on the 19th of November, 1942, we were a sad-looking bunch. Although about eighty of us had survived the journey in the boxcars, over the course of the next four days about half of the prisoners remaining prisoners died when we were finally fed. The weather was freezing and many of the prisoners suffered from frostbite due to the elements. My leg, which had been operated on in Camp Stutthoff, was in terrible shape, especially my right foot that had been operated on previously.

My foot hadn't received medical attention during the last ten or eleven days, and it showed evidence of gangrene settling in. They carried me from the train to a wagon. By wagon we were transported to the shower room for cleansing prior to taking us to the registration area in the camp. The showers had a steady flow of boiling hot water that was so hot we cringed in pain as the water burned our skin. Then they poured ice-cold water alternately to cool us down before again scalding us. Once the process was complete, the guards rushed us as a group to the area that had been designated for registering us into the camp.

As we approached the registration area, I could see long tables with officials sitting behind them. They had papers scattered in front of them, and the officials could be seen writing down information as the prisoners passed in front of them. It was at this location that I received a new prisoner number. Years later I learned that some camps issued prisoner numbers while other camps actually engraved the numbers in the skin. I was then assigned to Block 23, Room No. 2. The memories of the entire process were etched in my mind forever. The horror of what I was living through was so vivid that I still remember the details clearly.

Every prisoner was given a haircut during the registration process. The hair on our heads was cut very close to our scalp. They additionally shaved a two-inch strip of hair down the middle of our heads, and this hair-cutting procedure was continued on a weekly basis.

We were then issued our prison clothes, and we discovered that they were always either too small or too large. The clothing was usually tattered and dirty, too, as if it had been worn by others before us. Our clothes consisted of a pajama-like uniform with blue and white stripes. They sewed our prisoner number on the left side of our trousers and on the front left side of our lightweight shirt. To this uniform they again added the triangles we had received at the other camps. These were the triangles that indicated who was a Jew, who was a political prisoner, who was a religious fanatic, and so on.

It was at this introduction to the camp that a doctor came in to examine my foot before sending me to the barrack. He solemnly shook his head, and he paused only a moment before he said they would have to amputate my foot. It took only seconds for the shock to register as I realized what he was saying. I begged them not to. I told the doctor not to cut my foot off, that I would rather be dead than to be without a leg or a foot.

My plea must have touched the doctor's heart because I was shocked when he said he realized what I must have already gone through. Somehow, mercifully, my request was granted. He treated my foot with some medicine and salve and said he would see if it healed. At this point I felt mentally and physically exhausted.

At that point we were ushered to Block No. 23, our new home. It was located in the closed and restricted section of Camp Dachau. From this barrack, we could see prisoners being taken from the barracks to the gas chambers in the evening where they were first gassed and later their bodies were cremated. Sometimes it seemed like death would be our only escape from this wretched existence. Death seemed to be my constant companion and I felt as if I could smell it all around me.

24

Life at Camp Dachau

My early background had taught me that most people are very vulnerable and fragile. I came to realize that the prisoners who were still alive must have been tougher than I imagined. I myself would not have been able to survive this camp with these extreme conditions had there not been an inner strength or will to live. Yes, we all had our ups and downs. At times the sadness would feel overwhelming, and the daily routine and disruption of our lives was beyond the scope of imagination. Sometimes I felt like a corpse walking among the living dead.

I would look into the eyes of some of my fellow prisoners and sometimes only a hollow shell would return my gaze. It was easy to see the signs of hopelessness and depression and the tiredness of spirit that existed among the other men. I became extremely pale, and I felt very unhealthy. My weight had dropped to below one hundred pounds. I wondered if I could even survive any new illness. The lack of food was always foremost in my mind as my stomach rumbled continually. My skin became severely dry and started to feel like parchment.

It is unimaginable the way human beings treated other human beings.

Early in my stay at this camp, I was able to communicate with some of the prisoners beyond the fence, on the other side of the camp that was not restricted. They were able to walk about freely in their camp area, and two of them came over to the fence where I stood. They said they had heard about me and that I had survived the other camps. They tried to tell me about life on my side of the fence. They urged me to volunteer for any work that was available just to get out of the odd-numbered barrack I had been placed in. They warned me that the prisoners in the barrack were often chosen to be killed or taken off to be gassed.

So about a week later, when the German soldiers came to my barrack and asked for twenty volunteers, I quickly raised my hand. They took the group of volunteers away to the camp hospital. At the time I had no idea of where we were being taken or for what purpose. Thoughts raced through my head as we walked to the station that was known as the hospital. It didn't take long to discover our plight: the doctors said we had been chosen for a special important purpose. They were going to perform experiments with malaria to search for cures.

They ushered me to another room where they were going to give me an injection for that horrible disease. My thoughts raced with dread and uncertainty as I realized that they intended. I could feel my heart pounding in fear. When they stepped out to prepare the injection, I looked around for an opportunity to escape. Without hesitation I opened the window in the room and jumped out. I raced quickly back to my barrack. To my surprise, though, none of the other prisoners asked me what had happened.

I remained at this barrack as the winter came on with a vengeance. The temperatures were extremely cold, they would often reach well below zero and the winds would gust unmercifully. The guards enjoyed chasing the prisoners outside as a punishment. We were too lightly dressed for the extreme weather conditions, and everyone would stand outside shivering and trembling until the guards tired of their sport and let them return to the barrack. This became another form of torture, and the guards would look for the smallest infraction or sound that was uttered to play their cruel game.

25

A Memory of Christmas at Camp Dachau

The Christmas holidays had always been one of my favorite times of the year, and I had many warm memories of enjoying them with my family and friends. My memories had been special because it had always meant family members being together, lots of good food, laughter and a feeling of contentment and happiness. I used to look forward to the arrival of Christmas day with wonder and anticipation.

But in Concentration Camp Dachau, the holiday took on a different picture. One of my most vivid memories was of Christmas morning in 1942, when the prisoners were given fresh undershirts. Surprise was my first inclination, but that quickly changed to consternation. Within fifteen minutes several camp guards called loudly that there was going to be an inspection for lice. The guards picked out about twenty of the prisoners that included me and said that the shirts we had just received were suspected of having dry eggs.

We were herded outside into the freezing temperatures. I was trembling from the cold as the air struck me. The lightweight clothing I was wearing was no protection from the cold. My eyes watered and my feet almost refused to move as I felt the cold and wondered what would happen next. It wasn't long before I found out. The guards tortured us by dunking us in ice-cold water that had been placed in a huge tub. While we were shivering from the freezing water and dripping wet, the guards continued to throw buckets of freezing-cold water on us for what seemed an endless period of time. My group howled and screamed from the pain and unbearable torture.

This practice continued for more than an hour as we continued to scream in terror, standing in the cold and shivering uncontrollably. The prisoners from other blocks looked on helplessly. When I looked over at them, I could see frustration and pity in their faces. It was a Christmas day that was burned into my memory. I would often think back to that occurrence for years to come.

26

Work Detail in a New Barrack

In this camp, many of the work tasks we were assigned to were not much different from the other camps. Some prisoners were dispatched to the workshops and warehouses in the camp compound, while other prisoners were sent to work on maintenance and taking care of the custodial areas. Some prisoners were sent to nearby cities, to work in factories and shops that produced small arms, S.S. uniforms, and other commodities that were needed.

Thousands of prisoners in this compound were assigned to work in the Air Force and aviation industry in several of the nearby cities. The Praezifix, a factory in Dachau that manufactured airplane parts and screws, was known to have employed almost four hundred prisoners.

A few weeks later, I was assigned to work in barrack No. 2, with a small company called "Weberay." The tasks were simple and didn't take a lot of intricate knowledge to perform. It was obvious that we were working for a company that was profiting from the work we performed. The room was equipped with several tables and chairs, and there were four of us assigned to a table. The work we were accomplishing was putting together small parts for the company, with the Gestapo profiting from our labors.

Many of the priests had been assigned to work at this barrack, and I came to know several of them well. While working at Weberay, I was moved from block No. 23 and placed into block No. 18 where I was able to move around somewhat after work. Whenever the opportunity came up, I tried to visit the priests. I found our visits inspirational. When I returned to my barrack, I was left with a feeling of peace in spite of the horror of our imprisonment.

There was a huge crucifix that had been erected at the roadside in our camp. It loomed over the area and could be seen easily from many areas of the camp. It was common knowledge that reverence to the cross would be frowned on. In fact, if someone passing by greeted it or bowed in any way, they were severely punished and tortured with beatings. At times the person bowing would be singled out and have to remain on his feet for several days. He would not receive food or water for the entire time.

I knew that it was risky to practice my faith, that if I was caught there would be a severe punishment. Prisoners were known to be tortured, beaten, and sometimes shot just for doing what I was doing. I had known of people who had been thrown to the vicious dogs to be ripped apart. Any time a prisoner said something that was religious or tried to help a fellow prisoner, he would be severely beaten. Anything I did to practice my religion had to be done in secret.

Yet, knowing I could be killed didn't stop me. I would enter their barrack in the veil of darkness and find a chair somewhere near the shadow of a priest sitting there. I would kneel near him, make the sign of the cross, and say my confession. Then I would hand him a very small slice of bread I had managed to save from a meal. He would say a prayer and then bless it and hand it back to me. I would quickly swallow the bread and say a little prayer. This was my Holy Communion.

I had been raised from my childhood to go to church religiously, and I believed in God. It was my strong faith that had ultimately caused me to be elected as the president of the C.Y.O. (Catholic Youth Organization) in my village. Even in Camp Dachau, my belief and faith in God was unfailing. I tried to live my faith, though sometimes I would struggle with the reality of the horrifying conditions I was living with every day. I would question how a merciful God could let such brutality and savagery continue. But God was not the creator of the conditions. The Holocaust was the creation of evil men, it was evil that precipitated the terrible conditions and caused so many unconscionable deaths. When I prayed to God while in the camps, I would pray for guidance and inner strength to help me survive.

27

Priests in Camp Dachau

There were about two thousand priests in Camp Dachau. I learned that about four hundred and eighty of them were of Polish descent, and they came from a number of different countries: Holland, Italy, France, Poland, Yugoslavia, and Germany. Polish priests were often persecuted for two main reasons: because they were Poles and because they were Catholics. Priests of German origin numbered about three hundred and sixty. From 1940 until 1942 the priests were persecuted with a vengeance and treated very badly.

Priests would be seen working in labor groups with the other prisoners. Sometimes they were assigned in groups repairing roads, and some of them were used for pulling heavy wagons of coal and other material. In Camp Dachau, the older priests were usually harnessed to a roller and whipped by the guards to pull it along. Often the priests were given humiliating tasks and treated miserably. Some of them were sent to clean the gutters or wash the latrines. We could see them doing their jobs without complaint, sometimes having to carry excrement with their bare hands. I would witness the terrible way the priests were treated with frustration that I could do nothing to help them. I couldn't even help myself escape the captivity.

The camp leaders, capos and guards who were in charge, were often seen whipping them and beating them unmercifully. They were seen working barefoot because the guards delighted in seeing them suffer. Sometimes they would have to walk on gravel roads to get to their destination. I would feel a sense of helplessness when I saw their bleeding feet and realize the pain they must be suffering. Their dormitories were inspected constantly by the S.S. guards, who liked to find opportunities to inflict additional pain and suffering on them. They could expect to be visited by guards every hour on the hour.

The guards enjoyed inventing nasty pranks to humiliate the priests whenever an opportunity presented itself. Some of the younger S.S. Officers would bring their wolf dogs and incite them to charge like wild beasts at the priests as they completed their tasks. In spite of the constant indignities, many of the priests continued to ignore their personal hardship and struggle to fulfill the tasks assigned to them.

The priests were known to secretly celebrate mass because if they did it openly they would be killed. They received and distributed Holy Communion in dark hideouts, often risking their own safety and their lives as they dared to perform their sacred duties. I was thankful for the bravery of the priests because I was able to attend confession and mass several times while being imprisoned in the concentration camps. I even received Holy Communion whenever it was possible. I knew that if I was caught in these actions, it would mean the worst corporal punishment. I knew that it could even result in death.

I was fascinated with the magnificent show of contempt the priests made without thought of their own safety. Often they dared to perform their sacred duties almost under the very noses of the guards. Memories of the bravery of those fine individuals are burned in my mind forever. Every time I saw a priest I would mentally say a prayer for their safety.

Priests were often beaten savagely for the crime of hiding a rosary or a scapular. If a priest was seen making a sign of the cross or praying at any time, it meant immediate punishment and sometimes even death. Only the German priests were given special privileges. They were kept in a special dormitory and had a private chapel where they could celebrate mass throughout the war.

Then, in 1942 there were rumors going around that there had been Vatican intervention in the war effort. The pope had given a speech with positive statements about the German officials and that had changed everything. We noticed that the plight of priests took on a different look. They were no longer being given humiliating tasks and forced to work with the hard labor groups. They were allowed to do simple tasks and treated with more respect.

As far as I knew, the priests were kept primarily in Concentration Camp Dachau. Because the Vatican had showed support towards the German officials, it brought about a change in the feelings of the hierarchy. By 1943 the priests began to be treated with more leniencies and additional freedoms. They were given easier tasks to perform and treated with more respect. Guards were instructed to treat them less harshly than before.

28

Camp Life

In January of 1943 the Gestapo allowed prisoners to receive food parcels from home, but not many of the prisoners managed to get the parcels. If a prisoner was forced into a disciplinary squad, he was isolated from the other prisoners and was not able to write letters home or receive his food parcels. The prisoner being punished would be assigned difficult tasks, sometimes being forced to jump for hours or carry cement blocks up and down a stairway.

The capos, made up of German criminals or communist prisoners who had been mistreated by S.S. guards, would become the executioners of prisoners. They became the real master of each block or barrack, and they were able to choose their own aides or room guardians. They were able to inflict terrible punishments and tortures on the prisoners, even kill them if they wanted to.

In March of 1943 they took me to work in a plantation commando. There the prisoners who were unable to work or became too weak were beaten and tossed into a wagon. If a man felt exhausted, it was important that he not show how tired he felt. It was like a death sentence. Guards would beat anyone showing exhaustion until they were unconscious. Then their dead or almost dying bodies were carted off to gas chambers and later to the crematorium.

A vivid memory of Camp Dachau was the band that stood in the main area of the camp. Every day as we marched off to work, the band would play lively music like the German military march as our group was being marched off to our work detail. Some of the band members had accordions, violins, trumpets, and other instruments. It was difficult to believe that hearing beautiful music would be an accompaniment for our being marched off to hard labor.

Once at the job site, everyone had to work continuously and without slowing down. Sometimes the SS guards would watch prisoners working and write their number down for whatever reason suited their fancy. Our numbers were plainly visible on our coats and the side of our trousers.

As our prisoner group later returned back to camp, we would be detoured to the crematorium area and told to stop there. We would stop with trepidation, not knowing what was about to happen. Then the S.S. guard would come out and read off the numbers that had been selected, and those prisoners would have to step out from the group. They were taken inside, told to undress and lay their clothes neatly on the side. The group would then be pushed into the gas chambers.

Roll calls continued to be a part of our everyday routine. During roll calls, which took place at morning, noon, and in the evening in the square, the capos would walk among the rows of prisoners that had lined up. They would walk along and strike the healthy prisoners with their sticks. The sick or weak prisoners were laid on the ground, one next to another. The roll calls took place, in the pouring rain or in any kind of weather. They became a part of our everyday routine.

One roll call I remember especially well happened one day at about noon. That day something bad must have happened for the German occupation because the German Officers came out and said we would all be punished. Every tenth prisoner was going to be sent to the gas chamber, and we knew that meant death. As they began counting down the rows of prisoners, one of the prisoners who was chosen for death began crying loudly, pleading to be spared because he had a wife and small children.

I was surprised to see Bishop Michal Kozal step forward from his line and offer to be taken in place of the man who had been chosen. The German Officer agreed; but they took Bishop Kozal to a separate location, away from the prisoners being taken to the gas chambers. He was placed in a camp prison cell so he could die from starvation. He remained there without clothes and with no windows in his cell for more than two weeks. Some of the prisoners could hear him praying until he became very weak. I can still remember hearing him blessing the other victims of Nazi terror while praying.

After two weeks had passed, he didn't have much strength left in his body, but he was still alive. The German guards finally came, dragged him out of his cell, and killed him with an injection of carbolic acid. That priest was a saint; I have no qualms about that. I said a prayer for his soul, he died the death of a martyr.

There are other terrible memories of the experiments that were being carried out in the camp by S.S. doctors. Doctors often practiced sterilization methods on prisoners. Sometimes they would select prisoners who were fed only salt water to see how long they could survive. Other prisoners were subjected to freezing experiments where they were held in icy water or exposed naked in the now outdoors until they froze to death.

The doctors especially liked men in good physical condition to use for special research experiments. The men would become guinea pigs for new drugs and serums to be used against malaria and inflammatory tumors caused by malnutrition. Sometimes tests were performed on thousands of young men and women for research purposes.

Even more horrifying was the practice at this camp of using human skin for the manufacture of pocketbooks, lampshades, and countless other gruesome souvenirs. In some cases, prisoners who had unique tattoos on their bodies were kept on a special diet for a short time. When they had gained enough weight so their skin looked smooth, they then received a deadly dose of some poisonous drug. Prisoners were shot with poison bullets to see how long it took to kill them. There were experiments with mustard gas, injections with malaria, or injections with lethal doses of typhus and jaundice. Some prisoners were placed in pressure chambers and subjected to very high altitude tests until they stopped breathing. Some prisoners met their end by shootings, beatings, among other brutal tortures. They experimented with castration, or practiced performing operations.

I knew of a camp laboratory where they were procuring skulls and other human body parts. The parts were pickled in alcohol and then preserved. There were two S.S. doctors in charge of this laboratory, S.S. Doctor Adolf Pokorny and S.S. Doctor Rascher. They usually chose men with an unusually-shaped head to preserve them in the anatomical museum. Handsome young males and young girls with perfect bone structures had to die because nice skeletons were sought after by German universities.

29

Death Was All Around Us

A sick man who soiled his bunk was dragged to a washroom where male nurses poured a stream of cold water on his head until he died. If he refused to die quickly, the nurse would force a rubber pipe into his mouth, making him choke to death. The male nurses often delighted in kicking and clubbing their helpless victims. Sometimes they would torture victims by depriving them of their meager rations, keeping the rations for themselves instead. Male nurses helped the doctors inject the various poisons, or force the sick prisoners to swallow lethal pills.

The infirmary became known to the prisoners as a finishing chamber. In the beginning, no medical help was offered. The sick prisoners were simply left where they lay so they would ultimately die from illness or be taken off to a gas chamber.

The German S.S. officers had other ways to "finish" the sick. They would select prisoners in the barrack for extermination because they wanted to make room for healthier and more physically-fit men.

Every day a S.S. officer would make his rounds of the barrack to see the condition of the men. Those who looked weak were taken out and we knew they wouldn't be seen again.

In the Infirmary, the selection was even faster. The Komandant himself would visit the sick and dying. He would arrive every week and walk around the beds where the men lay. He usually had a pleasant manner about him and came with a charming smile. He greeted the sick, approaching each bed and bestowing kind words of sympathy. While he chatted with the prisoners who were able to talk, he would inquire pleasantly about their health, asking them if they were married. He inquired about how many children were waiting for "daddy" at home. When the prisoner answered "Four kids," the Komandant would smile broadly and say, "That's nice; they are waiting for you to come home."

As he walked away from the bed he smiled again to show how pleasant he was while he was already writing on a paper the number of the prisoner. Later, all the numbers he had written down were given to S.S. guards to be taken to the gas chambers for extermination.

As diseases, like typhus, spread through the camps, more and more prisoners became sick. But the sick prisoners would pretend that they were still healthy enough to work. They knew that being sick meant death. The only resistance the prisoners could offer to the inhumane treatment was staying alive.

Sometimes in the Infirmary, a S.S. officer would arrive and read off a list of names. The people on the list were ordered to disrobe, leaving their shirts. They were sent to the operating hall. No one ever returned from such a trip. The operation was a simple one. One injection of quicksilver, and death came instantly. Because we knew what usually occurred in these situations, often the victim who was selected had to be removed forcibly.

I recall another time when officers came into our barrack and selected more than 5,000 prisoners for a transport to another camp. We later learned that they had been sent to a gas chamber in a camp near Linz.

A single crematorium was used to burn more than a thousand corpses a day. Prisoners being forced into trucks to take them to the gas chambers often knew where they were being sent. Yet they didn't utter a word of protest. They would depart, smiling, as if going out on a pleasure trip. Many times I heard men say, "If there is a God, why does he allow such crimes to be committed?" But I said that if God did everything we wanted him to do, he would be our servant. I still continued to believe in God, and I believed that the day would come when justice would be done.

Living conditions continued to be terrible. There was no privacy while we worked or slept. Our sleep period was generally reduced to about five or six hours. Exhaustion caused many deaths over time. Conditions continued to deteriorate. The prisoners had poor medical care; there were only a limited number of latrines. There was overcrowding in every block. There was inadequate clothing for the weather conditions.

The filthy conditions that were compounded by starvation lowered the resistance of many prisoners to disease. I watched as fellow prisoners became ill and died because they couldn't cope with the life we had to live. In some cases, I saw men become so despondent about their lives that they would run outside and beg the S.S. Guards to shoot them. Of course, the guards were usually very happy to oblige. I can still remember seeing them smile as they killed the poor victims.

If prisoners were unable to keep up a good pace in their routines, they were either executed on the spot or simply scheduled for extermination. For even the smallest infraction of camp regulations, a group of ten or twelve prisoners would be removed from their quarters and asked what kind of death they preferred. They could choose between being hanged or shot. After 30 minutes of grace, they were forced to strip and then executed by the method they had selected.

Sometimes the S.S. guards didn't give the prisoners a choice. They simply took a group of men to a vacant site on a cold winter night, forced them to strip, and hosed them with cold water. In the morning a labor detail would be sent out to collect their bodies. Or, if it was a larger group, they would be taken to the crematorium and executed, for the sake of convenience.

Life at the camp continued from day to day, sometimes we were taken on other details with different jobs assigned to us. Our camp was situated near an airplane factory that was hidden by diversions that had been contrived by the German guards. The guards had placed barrels around the perimeter of the building. Those barrels were filled with a substance that would create a fog when planes entered the airspace above the factory. The end result was that the planes finally had to bomb everything in the area because they couldn't get a clear view of their target.

I learned that when the area around the factory was bombed, we were kept like hostages. While we worked on the rockets, sometimes I would learn more about our surroundings. One of the German engineers who worked with us told me that the company that owned this factory had bought us (the prisoners) to do the work as slaves. We were still maintained by the Gestapo, but owned by the company. I knew, too, that if the factory was bombed, we would simply be sent to another location to make the rockets.

One night in March of 1943 I was working on the nightshift. It was about one o'clock in the morning, and I was working on a machine near the office. While I worked, I noticed that the German obersharfuehrer who was in charge of our group had fallen asleep by his desk; and I could see him clearly from the window where I was standing. At the same time I could see that three German officers who were in charge of the entire camp had walked into the factory and were headed toward the sleeping officer. Quickly I realized there would be consequences if he were discovered asleep. He was in danger of being severely punished, and that meant possible transfer to another location.

Several thoughts raced through my mind. I recognized that the obersharfuehrer was known for treating prisoners fairly. I paused only for an instant before I decided to wake him up. I took a small wet rag and threw it in the window so it fell near him. Surprised, he raised his head up and looked at the window where I stood. I pointed to him that three top officers were coming. He quickly jumped to his feet as I signaled where the officers were. As they approached his office, he was already on his feet and able to greet them.

Once the officers had left, I saw him give a visible sigh of relief. I felt certain he knew I had saved his neck. He took his lunch bag with food in it, and placed it quietly on my chair near the machine I was working on. He pointed at the bag and at me, indicating that it was for me.

30

Destruction of the Camp

One night in April of 1943 our camp was bombed so badly that everything in the area was burning. About fifteen hundred prisoners were killed immediately, and the prisoners who had escaped immediate death began scattering about the compound in fright. The S.S. guards began circling the area with their machine guns raised, as if ready to shoot at any provocation. The picture of the buildings in the entire area blasted to smithereens was an ominous sight.

The S.S. guards started yelling loudly so they could be heard over the roar of the flames as bombs continued to fall. They told us to run to the gate so they would let us out. The entire camp was in chaos and a few of the prisoners were attempting to climb the fences to get out. Everyone else believed the words of the guards, and started running in the direction of the gate. Shouts could be heard among the prisoners, frightened voices saying, "Head for the gate. Get to the main gate."

As fire raged everywhere, I realized that my path was blocked by the flames and that I would have to somehow get through the inferno that raged directly in front of me. I grabbed a blanket that was lying on the ground and wrapped it around me and jumped into the cement pit that we had built earlier on one of our work details for protection from bombings. Since it was filled with water, I was soon soaking wet. I shivered in my wet clothes, though I believe it was more from fright than from the coldness of the water. Still holding tightly to the wet blanket, I ran through the flames and toward the main gate.

As I neared the other prisoners, I noticed that everyone was being herded into a group and that the guards had positioned themselves in a circle that surrounded them. I noticed, too, that the guards had their big machine guns aimed at the group. They yelled for everyone to kneel down, and to my shock and horror I realized that the guards were not planning to let anyone escape.

With an urgency I didn't know I possessed, I scrambled behind one of the brick posts that were off to my side. The guards commenced shooting, and the prisoners kneeling in front were killed immediately. It was a miracle that I had been able to stay alive. Just a few seconds later, as the guards continued shooting, a bomb fell directly on top of the machine guns at the gate and killed the S.S. guards.

The prisoners that hadn't been killed began running toward the kitchen bunker where food was kept in storage. I ran with them, and we found just one older S.S. guard watching over the area. He appeared to be in a daze and didn't say a word. He just stood there looking at us. I believe he was frightened himself.

We all grabbed some food from the bunker, salami, some bread, and whatever food we could get our hands on; and we ran back outside. We hid in the ditches around the barracks. There were actually no barracks remaining, they had burned to the ground. We stayed in those ditches for the next two days, trying not to move about and sleeping when we could. We managed to remain hidden while we waited to see what would happen next.

As we expected, the German guards returned to the camp area. All of us were gathered together, but our pace as we struggled to our feet and crawled out of the ditch was very slow. Our exhaustion was plainly visible as we stumbled to the clearing. We were a bedraggled crew, everyone's face looked haunted. The guards made us pick up the dead corpses and lay them out in a line. They were counted along with the living to make sure no one had managed to escape. The entire camp was short of food and water. Living conditions were almost impossible, the camp had been destroyed. I felt as if we were living through a nightmare, and I wondered where the next episode would lead us.

The destruction of the camp led to our transfer to another camp where our sad journey would continue. Together with many of the remaining prisoners I was transferred to Friedrichshafen, the Dachau Ousentcommando at Saulgau.

31

Camp Friedrichshafen

Thus it was that in the spring of 1943 I was sent to an Ousen commando in Friedrichshafen near Switzerland. The camp belonged to Dachau and held about three thousand prisoners. This prison camp was similar to the others in the way the guards treated the prisoners. We were treated like animals without regard to our comfort or feelings. Every prisoner was constantly punished for without provocation, and their handling of the barrack was very strict.

When we first arrived at this concentration camp, every prisoner had their hair sheared close to their head as it had in the other camps. Through the middle of our heads there was still the two-inch-wide strip that felt strange and uncomfortable. I learned much later during my captivity that the reason for this "look" was so a prisoner would be easily noticed if he tried to escape the camp.

It was a fact of life that it didn't take long for prisoners to become fed up with the routine of camp life and the terrible treatment received by the guards. There was equal hatred of the work details where prisoners were sent to work in the factories. It was mentally and physically challenging to live each day in fear of punishment and death. Often the prisoners would talk among themselves and try to discover ways to make an escape. But at the same time, everyone knew that it was futile to try to escape. We had learned from experience that it was not a good idea to attempt to escape because the only known way out of this camp was Death.

In the beginning of my stay at this camp, I was assigned to perform cement work. I was placed on a work detail that was designated to build cement bunkers. The purpose was to protect the machines from being damaged when the factory was bombed. This camp was bombed quite often, and much of our preliminary work at the camp involved the preparation of the cement for the bunkers.

The German officials in charge wanted to protect the machines in the camp because other camps had been bombed over the past few months. For a period of time I was assigned to work with a number of other prisoners to erect bunkers around the machines that were inside the factories. They even tried to protect the outside areas in the camp, the areas between the barracks, to avoid total destruction of the camp.

32

Attempted Escape from Prison Camp

Many of the jobs we were assigned to involved working in the huge factory that was nearby. The factory was a much-hated and dreaded place to have to work in. But in desperation, plans for escape were born in the strangest of places. It was in the factory that a few prisoners decided to make an escape attempt.

Inside the factory there was a big latrine in one corner which about twenty prisoners would have to use at any given time. Inside the latrine, off to one side, was a wall that was about two-feet high and there was a beam about six by eight inches in diameter that ran across it. The workers would have to sit on the beam to take care of their personal needs. There was water on one side of the beam, where the waste would fall, and on the other side there was a big pipe about two feet in diameter. The pipe was used to carry the waste out to the sewer areas.

It was this latrine that two of the prisoners in my barrack used to plan their escape. While working in the factory, they said they had to go to the bathroom. Once inside the latrine, they left their shoes near the wall of the latrine and jumped in with the human waste. They were hoping to make it out somewhere through the sewer area where the pipe reached.

They probably would have been able to succeed in their attempt without even being noticed except for one small detail. Their shoes that were left behind at the side of the latrine were the only thing that brought their escape attempt to the notice of the guards. No one would have believed that prisoners would have been willing to wade through with human waste in a pipe that was barely big enough to carry a human being. It was almost unthinkable. The men must have pushed through with their heads while using their feet to mobilize themselves through the very narrow and tightly-fitting pipe.

When the guards noticed the shoes in the latrine, they quickly realized that the prisoners were missing. They called some of the other guards in the area to help them in their search. They followed the pipe outside the factory to where the waste materials were left off. It went for quite a distance from the factory.

As the guards rushed alongside the pipe, they pulled out their guns and began shooting in desperation, almost in frenzy. They kept shooting through the pipe in anger, trying to hit anything that was moving. When they reached the end of the pipe, they searched the area diligently to try to discover the whereabouts of the prisoners who were missing, but we never learned of the outcome. If they were found, the guards didn't let us know. I often wondered if the desperate men had been able to reach safety and finally manage an escape from the horrible existence.

Everyone in the factory was punished for their escape. As the guards searched for the missing men, every prisoner in the factory had to stand at attention for more than four hours while they continued the search in desperation. This method of escape was not attempted again.

33

Winter of Cold and Desperation

The winter months in Camp Friedrichshafen were extremely cold. The temperatures would reach unbearable temperatures. Sometimes the S.S. guards would take us out in groups to gather some dry wood from the forest. They would take a couple of big wagons that were like trailers that could carry huge quantities of heavy wood, and they would harness us to the front of the wagons. The guards would expect the weak and prisoners who were freezing from the cold temperatures to pull those heavy wagons on the journey back to the camp grounds.

At the site of the wooded area, the prisoner detail was expected to quickly gather the wood and load it onto the trailers. Many of the men were exhausted from lugging the heavy wood logs. The exhaustion was terrible, but it became even worse as we were then made to pull the wagon that was now even heavier back to camp.

The journey back to camp was unbearable and many of the prisoners never made it back to the camp. We were forced to pull those heavy wagons for more than three miles while the S.S. guards hovered over us to see that we didn't try to escape. I could feel my muscles tense from the heaviness of the harness, and I wondered if I had the endurance to make it back to camp.

The entire time that the load was being pulled, the guards would relentlessly strike and beat every prisoner to try to make them move faster. They laughed at our struggle to move the heavy load, and they jeered at the prisoners who became weak and stumbled. If a man fell to his knees from weakness, he was whipped and struck with a club to get him moving again. We were treated like animals, without any regard for human life.

The bitter cold of the winter months made working even more difficult for many of the prisoners. The light clothing gave little protection from the weather conditions and many of the men suffered from frostbite because they didn't even have socks for their feet. Sometimes the cold would cause dizzy spells or fingers would go numb from the very low temperatures.

One of my many terrible memories of this camp was of the guards shouting at us to hurry, that we weren't going fast enough. Often their shouts would be filled with loud cursing as they urged the prisoners to increase their speed. They would shout to pull the wagon faster, faster.

The sight of their bull-whips swinging in the air as they jeered and shouted loudly is still vivid in my mind as I remember the cold winter months and the terrifying cruelty that seemed to have no end. The guard details even had vicious dogs that were used to keep the prisoners moving. It is a picture that has been imprinted in my mind forever.

34

An Idea Was Born
to Find Warmth

The weather continued to be bitter cold. Though we had a small stove in our barracks at this camp, we discovered that the wood we had carted back to the camp was not intended for our comfort. The guards used the wood from the wagons for their own use and for their own comfort. It became necessary for us to find other ways to heat our barrack.

If we found pieces of wood on our way to or from our work assignments, we would pick it up and hide it in our clothing or in our shoes. In that way we could bring it back to the barrack for use in our stove without the guards noticing. But it was really difficult to find enough wood to make a difference. It became a real struggle to keep ourselves warm.

Our barrack was near a barbed-wire fence that had a small gate and a larger gate. The larger gate was usually locked, but we soon saw that the small gate was left open with a S.S. guard usually guarding it from about 5 o'clock in the morning until 8 o'clock at night. The gate was near the kitchen, and we knew that the cooks were preparing coffee kettles there in the morning to be taken to the barracks. We also knew that at the side of the kitchen there was a shed that was filled with coal that the S.S. guards used in their barracks to keep themselves warm.

The bitter cold finally tempted us to plan an attempt to try to get some of the coal for our stove. Our plan was to go out early in the morning, before the S.S. guard came, and pass through the gate. We would grab as much coal as we could carry and try to quickly return to our barrack. That would help us stay warm.

Everyone in our room agreed to take part, and we prepared small bags to carry the coal. But then the question came up about who would go first. No one seemed willing to be the first, so I volunteered. I reasoned to myself that when everyone went into the shed to get the coal they might make even small noises and possibly be caught. The other prisoners agreed that I would lead the way and they would follow close behind.

On a cold morning, not long after we talked, we were able to put our plan into action. Very early in the morning we woke before the guard had arrived and went through the fence like geese following each other. I went first, and the prisoner who was directly behind me got inside the shed and we quickly filled our bags with the coal. We started to return to our barracks as the other prisoners were following our steps into the shed for their turn at the coal.

Just then I noticed that the S.S. guard had arrived early for his shift. I was filled with trepidation as I saw him standing at the gate. I signaled to the prisoner with me that we should go into the kitchen. I saw the kettles filled with coffee, so I got an idea. We both put our bags of coal in the bottom of two of the kettles and we lugged them to the gate.

When the S.S. guard expressed surprise that we were there, we told him we had gone through just before he arrived, and we were taking the kettles to the barracks. The guard let us go through, and we went as quickly as we could to a nearby washroom to dump the coffee. We took our bags with the coal and returned to our barrack.

Using the coal we brought in, we quickly started a fire and began warming ourselves. As the other prisoners shuffled in, they expressed surprise that we had managed to return with the coal. They had been caught by the guard as they tried to get through with their bags of coal, and they had been beaten badly. When we told them about our idea to use the coffee kettles, they said they wished they had thought of it too!

It was sad to think, though, that if they had been caught with coal at a camp in Dachau or Stutthoff, they would have been shot on the spot, not just beaten. It's funny how you think of the strangest things at moments like this. But I had discovered that the guards at this camp were not as strict as the guards at the other camps. They needed prisoners to work, so instead of killing prisoners for an infraction, they were usually beaten instead.

In fact, our living quarters were better than the previous camp because of the need to keep the prisoners working. We had smaller rooms in the barracks, and there were fewer prisoners to each room. We had twenty-six prisoners in our room and we ran it pretty much by ourselves. Our work at the factory consisted of two 12-hour shifts, and each shift was managed by a Shafuhrer and one Obersharfuehrer.

35

Work at Camp Friedrichshafen

This camp was especially designed to work on the erection of a new factory in which V-1 and V-2 rockets would be worked on. I was then put to work as a welder, using an electric punch-welding machine. My job was to weld the outside shields together. Sometimes I worked doing cement work, too, carrying bricks in a transporting column. One time I remember seeing a German civilian engineer come to our station and complain that some of the prisoners were working too slowly. The Obersharfuehrer replied, "You just leave them alone and it will be alright." That's how I knew we were being treated more leniently at this camp.

I tried to do the work as ordered though the tortures still continued. I was often beaten, clubbed, and kicked severely by the S.S. guards. The capos at this camp were especially cruel, making the lives of all the prisoners a terrifying torture every day.

The camp was located not far from the factory we were working in. And we were bombed frequently, sometimes during the day and sometimes at night. While working in the factory, when planes were approaching to drop their bombs, the prisoners were forced to enter a shallow tunnel that was five feet by four feet under the floor. We would struggle to breathe from the lack of air. The S.S. guards, though, made sure they were protected from danger. They had concrete bunkers build right near the tunnel door where they could run quickly for safety.

The twelve-hour shifts we worked on seemed endless and exhausting. On Sundays we were given a break from working at the factory. Instead, they would transport us to bombed areas where we were made to take the bombed buildings apart. If a prisoner managed to escape, the remaining prisoners were forced to remain standing at attention until the escapee had been recaptured or found. Sometimes when we were out standing on the road in the mud, the S.S. commandant would pull up and yell, "Hihlaygane" (which meant 'lay down'). If a prisoner was too slow to respond, he was quickly shot. And bombings were a frequent occurrence. Sometimes I wondered if the world had gone mad or simply insane.

36

Occasional Squabbles in the Barrack

Life in the barrack in Camp Frederickson changed over time. In the beginning the guards were very strict and our work hours were exhausting and very long. Gradually, though, conditions were eased a little to get the prisoners to work harder. I was surprised as the rules became less rigid and the officers in charge seemed to relax in their overall treatment of our barrack.

There were eight rooms in our barrack, and there were four entrances. In the room I was in, there were twenty-six prisoners being housed. The Stube-elster, the staff member in charge of our area, directly controlled what went on in the barrack, but the Blockelster, the German staff member who oversaw everything, came to us one day. He hadn't been interfering with our lives and had a new directive for us.

He told us that each room should select one person from among the prisoners to be in charge of the group. That person would be in control over who was sent to bring the coffee or soup from the kitchen, or generally control the room positions. In my room, there were mostly Polish prisoners, with a few Hungarians, a few Serbs, a few French, and one German Catholic. The German prisoner spoke good Polish, and we all managed to communicate with each other.

They chose me to be in charge of the room. We had been getting along well and struggled with our existence together, often commiserating with each other about the hopelessness of our situation. At first we worked well together as I selected people in turn to get the coffee or tea and other meals to bring to our group.

It was surprising, therefore, one day in April of 1944 when I sent two of our men to bring a kettle of tea from the kitchen. I passed out the tea to everyone, making certain everyone had a serving. Finally, I noticed that there was just a little tea left in the kettle so I asked if anyone wanted the remainder. No one seemed to want the rest, so the German prisoner came up to me and asked if he could have the rest. I put what was left in his cup, and he saved it by putting it on the stove in our room to keep it warm.

After a half hour went by, two of the Polish prisoners walked over to him and grabbed his cup of tea. He quietly told them, "That is my tea." They angrily turned to him and started beating him. Seeing what was happening, I quickly stepped in between them to try to stop the altercation.

"It's his tea." I said. "Leave him alone, you didn't want it before, and now it's his."

They became very angry at my words and turned to me. "Why are you defending a German?" they asked. Again I responded that the tea was his and told them to leave him alone. I reminded them that he was a prisoner just like the rest of us. My words seemed to infuriate them even more though we had never had any problems getting along in the past.

One of the Polish prisoners then grabbed a hammer that was lying near the stove and shook it menacingly at me as he looked at the other Polish prisoner. "Should I give it to him?" he asked as he shook the hammer in my face.

"Hit him!" the other Polish prisoner shouted. At that verbal command, the prisoner with the hammer struck me with all his strength, hitting the left side of my forehead with the hammer. I fell to the floor, bleeding from my head, and struggled to defend myself. The other prisoners in the room saw what was happening and tried to intervene.

They managed to pull the prisoner with the hammer away from me as the other prisoners helped me to the medical station. Luckily, there was a doctor available and he was able to see me right away. After looking me over, he patched up my forehead; they had actually punctured a hole in my forehead with the hammer, and he managed to stop the bleeding. The doctor asked if I wanted to report the incident, but I decided against it. I felt we were all frustrated with the hopelessness of the camp situation, and I didn't want to get anyone in trouble.

The doctor shook his head in disbelief. "The hole in your head will heal eventually," he said. "You'll probably have a scar afterwards, though. Tell people that a part of a bomb hit you in the head and the scar is your souvenir."

Upon returning to our room, I announced to everyone that I no longer wanted to be in charge. I was frustrated with the situation and didn't want to handle such situations again. For a few days, no one went to bring the tea. Finally, a few prisoners went out and brought some on their own. Several times they tried to talk me into being in charge again, but I refused.

After several days, the other prisoners started talking about what had occurred, and they were criticizing the Polish prisoners who had caused the injury to me. But our camp was bombed badly right about this time, and many prisoners didn't survive the bombing.

37

Memories of Camp Friedrichshafen

There were frequent bombings when planes would come into the area and just drop their bombs throughout the camp. We would listen to the peal of the alarm that would sound just before they hit. It was a frightening sound, and it was a sound I had become accustomed to at this camp.

In October of 1943 I was still working on the night shift. There was one particular day that I was asleep in my barrack because of the late working hours when the alarm sounded that the planes were coming to bomb us. Jumping out of my bunk in a rush, I went outside as quickly as I could. My only thought was to find safety.

The front of the camp seemed to be a logical answer because I knew there was a big strong bunker there that had two big metal doors. I ran to the entrance on the left side, door No. 1, and was just about to enter when I noticed some S.S. guards running in that door.

So I turned quickly to the right and ran to door No. 2. I thought that if the bomb hit us directly I didn't want to die with them. The entrance was crowded with other prisoners trying to get in. Just as I made it inside, a bomb fell at the entrance of door No. 1, and almost everyone in that area was killed. For a while I felt dumb with shock. I said a little prayer of relief, my instinct had been correct. In my effort not to die with the S.S. guards, I had been saved. The people who had run into the second door had managed to survive.

On another occasion in February of 1944 I was working on the night shift at around 11 o'clock in the evening. Suddenly I heard the alarms go off, signaling that the planes were coming to drop bombs. There were no bunkers in the immediate area for the prisoners, but there were some small tunnels nearby that were used for pipes and wires to pass through. The tunnels were about four feet wide and five feet high, with very little passing space available. There was also a small bunker for a S.S. guard to hide.

Several of the prisoners rushed to the tiny tunnel, scrambling for a safe haven. I climbed inside, but it was very crowded. There was very little space to move around because it was a tight fit. There we remained for about a half an hour. There was very little air, and we had trouble breathing as it became more stifled.

If the bomb had hit us directly, I'm certain we would all have been killed on the spot, but luckily we survived. When the bombing ended, the S.S. guards opened the door to our tunnel and found us gasping for air. As I looked up from where I stood, I could see that the roofs were gone. The factory we had been working in was demolished, nothing remained of the structure we had known just an hour before. They ushered the remaining prisoners back to the main camp area that hadn't been bombed. My only thought was that we had survived.

And there was one time early in the spring of 1944 that stands out. I was again working nights so when eleven o'clock rolled around I was fast asleep in my bunk. I woke to the sound of loud sirens. I jumped from the bunk and ran to the window to see what was going on. As a rule, we weren't allowed to look out the window. But there was a table standing by the window, and I was able to look underneath the table to see some of the commotion outside. The top of our barrack had a post with a flag and artillery to shoot planes down.

As I was looking up towards the sky, I could see a big bomber plane coming down straight toward our barrack. My first instinct was to run. I was sure a bomb was about to be dropped right on top of us. I jumped out the window and ran toward a huge hole that was made into a basement for a washroom. It had pipes there and one faucet that provided water. Someone must have been using it recently because it was left on, still running, and the water was very cold. Without further thought, I jumped into that hole that was already filled with water to hide from the bombs. I almost drowned in the water; I hadn't realized how deep it was.

I discovered later that the plane had been flying very low because it had been damaged and was in serious trouble. It had been about to crash, and the pilot was coming down rapidly as he was trying to reach the border at Switzerland. Our camp just happened to be in his path just near the border. It wasn't until much later, after we had been liberated, that I happened to read about the pilot in a *Reader's Digest* article in the April 1993 issue. The article was entitled, "On a Wing and a Prayer" and told about what had occurred on that fateful day.

The pilot was Lt. Jack Elliott and his B-24 bomber plane had been shot down in the area I had been in. I learned that he had been targeting the armaments plants in Friedrichshafen, Germany, when his plane was hit. He had survived the crash and been hidden on the edge of France, where it meets Germany and Switzerland.

Memories of this camp included several times that we were bombed and had to be moved to other locations until the debris could be taken care of. I vividly remember the time the camp was being divided into two groups. One group of prisoners was to be sent to Lintz and Maurenhasen somewhere near Austria. The second group of prisoners would be sent to Saulgau.

I stood silently between both groups as they were being prepared for transport. I didn't know what direction I should take. Neither choice of groups was to my liking. I wondered what fate intended for me and if death would be the outcome if I made the wrong choice. While I stood deep in thought, I noticed that the prisoners standing nearest to me were the two Polish prisoners who had fought with me over my defense of the German prisoner. They pleaded with me to stay with the prisoners from our barrack and come in their group. They had decided to go to Lintz. They hugged me and said they respected me and believed I had always treated them fairly. But somehow instinct told me that I shouldn't go. Call it a gut feeling, or just a fleeting moment, but I made a sudden decision.

Though I knew that Saulgau was known to have bad conditions, for some unknown reason I had a feeling that I should not go to Lintz. It was after I had chosen Saulgau and managed to stay alive that I learned that the group of prisoners who were scheduled for Lintz had been instead taken to the gas chambers for extermination. I felt tremors of shock go through me as I realized the prisoners I had known were all dead.

I arrived in the concentration camp in Saulgau on April 26, 1944. The camp was about forty miles north. This was also an Ousen commando that belonged to Camp Dachau. The city of Saulgau is just north of Friedrichshafen and about half way to Dachau.

38

Saulgau, Back at Concentration Camp Dachau

Saulgau was a small town and their prison camp was located not far from the factories. The camp belonged to Concentration Camp Dachau and was at the very outskirts of the small town. I learned very soon after our arrival that this camp was much stricter than the last camp had been.

Upon arriving at this new camp, I was scheduled to work on machines that were similar to the work I had been doing in the other camp. The machines were making V-I and V-II rockets. Again I worked as an electric punch-welding machine operator. While talking with one of the civilian German engineers on one occasion, he told me that the company that made the bombs had actually bought the prisoners from the German prison authorities to work for them. But the prisoners still remained under the supervision of the Gestapo and the S.S. soldiers from Dachau.

On one occasion I was working on a spot-welding machine. As I finished a section of the rocket I was working on, I noticed that one punch mark was burned. When the German inspector came by and started checking out the work with a magnifying glass, I pretended that I was reaching for something and covered the area with my hand. The inspector looked around and approved my work with his stamp as was his usual routine.

In a few hours the guards returned to tell me that I had spoiled one section of the rocket, that my work was bad. Immediately I stepped to the front of the rocket and showed them the stamp of approval by the German inspector. That stamp had saved me from being punished. I knew I could have been shot or hung for doing bad work.

The frequent punishments and daily work routine continued as the months passed. Soon it was winter and the temperatures were freezing and unbearable. We had to work without coats. I suffered from frostbite as we were transported to load the boxcars with the V-1 bombs. The routine of the work was depressing, and I longed to let my family know about my situation even though I realized that it was forbidden to write letters to anyone. I managed to acquire an envelope and paper, and I wrote a note to my parents telling them that I was still alive and was praying that I would somehow survive my captivity.

One day after we had finished our work detail, the prisoners were being returned back to camp. As our group passed through the town of Saulgau, I threw the envelope with my note toward the mailbox on our path. I hoped someone would see it on the ground and drop it in the mailbox. Unfortunately, the envelope was noticed by the camp komandant. This fact was brought to my attention the very next morning when his secretary came to escort me to the komandant's office.

As soon as I entered his office I knew I was in trouble. There was a pistol on his desk, and I could see his hand placed lightly on it as he glared at me. "Did you mail a letter yesterday?" he asked.

I realized it would be futile to lie or pretend innocence. I nodded my head up and down slowly. "Yes, I did," was my reply. I thought quickly as I stood there. Going against the rules and mailing a letter resulted in instant death. What could I do to save myself? At that moment, I remembered that one of the officers had just yesterday been shipped off to the Russian front for punishment. "But I had permission from the officer in charge." I named him quickly, knowing he wasn't available for confirmation.

Then I pointed at the secretary who was sitting at his desk near the komandant's office. In surprise at my words, the secretary shook his head in affirmation. "Yes," he said. "I heard him get permission."

Relief flooded through me as I realized that I had been able to escape death once again. I didn't escape punishment, though. The komandant pushed the pistol away as he stood up abruptly. He assigned me to a difficult work detail for the next few weeks to set an example that mail couldn't be sent out.

It was during this time that news filtered into the camp about the American invasion in Sherburg, France. Everyone in the camp was talking about the invasion, and there were hopes that liberation would soon be on the horizon. We felt excitement in the air, and everyone had strong hopes that something was about to happen.

About three weeks later, while at roll call, I was standing in the front row when the camp komandant came through for inspection. When he heard someone whispering, he thought it had come from my direction so he approached in my direction menacingly. He stopped directly in front of me and stared at me.

After a minute had passed, he gruffly said, "Why are you whispering, you're happy that the Americans landed?" Then he slapped me really hard on both sides of my face. His face looked hateful and filled with contempt. Still very angry, he started to kick me in the stomach with all his might, sending me reeling to the ground. As suddenly as the attack started, he stopped and left me lying there. I struggled to get up from the ground not knowing if he would strike me again. At that point we were all dismissed and sent back to our barrack.

39

Problem of Lice

In this camp, as in the previous concentration camps, there was a serious problem of lice in the barracks. Many of the prisoners suffered from the problem, and it was difficult to avoid exposure to it. I did everything I could to keep myself as clean as possible, though it wasn't easy with the terrible conditions we lived in. I had read about the problem of lice while still at home and knew a few helpful techniques for avoiding the problem.

While I worked in the factory that had the machines for building rockets, I was able to lay my hands on benzene. It was just like gasoline, and I realized it could be useful to me. I took a piece of rag and dipped it in the gasoline-like substance and used it to rub down my entire pajama-like outfit. I smelled of gasoline, but I believed it was worth suffering the odor to avoid the problem of lice. When I went to the barrack, the substance kept the lice of the other prisoners away from me as well because they avoided me.

40

The Hole

There were more than two thousand prisoners being held in the concentration camp in Saulgau. It was a large camp that had some features that stuck out in my memory. One of them was a man-made feature that caused dread and apprehension in everyone. Every prisoner knew about the huge deep hole that had been dug out with a horrifying purpose in mind. The hole was about forty feet long by twenty feet wide, which was a frightening sight. It was also about fifteen feet deep.

Everyone knew that the hole was especially prepared for us. We knew it was there to bury us in case of Germany's defeat. Yes, everyone knew it, but we lived with the gruesome knowledge. And we continued to wait and pray for a miracle to occur so the hole would never have to be used.

That hole was a constant reminder that Death would be our only way out of the camp. Escape was practically nonexistent. Every time we passed by the hole, I would look at it and wonder if I would become one of the bodies that would one day fill that empty space. It was a horrible feeling, knowing how fragile life is and how fate alone would determine when a person ceased to exist.

41

A Personal Experience at Dachau

Time continued to march forward. The drudgery of our daily existence and our struggle to survive kept pace without change. The winter was very cold, and I can remember working on the day shift one time especially. It was freezing as I worked on the spot-welding machine that was near a wall. There was a stove inside our factory that was usually burning and several of the other prisoners would sneak up to the stove to try to warm up.

The Komanderfurer who was in charge of our entire group was very strict, though, and we knew he was always ready to beat anyone who got in his way. He would chase the prisoners from the stove and shove them back to work, kicking them or beating them in the process. He walked through the factory to where I was working on my machine and asked me, "How come I never see you running to the stove?"

I replied, "It's stupid to run to the stove, get hot for just a few minutes, and then go back to freeze some more."

He smiled, which was rare, looked at me and said, "You are right." After that brief conversation I noticed that he tended to leave me alone so I could do my work in peace.

About two weeks later, I was working on the midnight shift. That day our camp had been bombed during the day, and the prisoners who were loading the V-1 rockets on the train were unable to load them onto the boxcars because of the bombings. We were told not to report to work that night and that only a group of about sixty of us would remain to load the rockets onto the boxcars. The other prisoners would go back to camp to sleep. The Komanderfurer from our shift was put in charge of selecting who would remain to work loading the bombs into the boxcars and who would be sent back to camp to sleep. He looked at me, smiled, and said, "Go to camp and sleep."

Each group of prisoners also had a clerk who kept the names of the prisoners in the group. He acted like a big-shot, believing himself to be very important. As I returned to our room and prepared to go to sleep, I heard him complaining about me to another German guard who was in charge of our room. He said he had to call me several times to work and that I had been slow to respond.

When the guard mentioned to him that I was in the room getting ready to sleep, he became enraged and started towards me. I told him that the Komanderfurer had told me to return to camp, but he ignored my words as if he didn't care. As he reached me, he started swinging at me with his fists. I bent down to avoid his blow and his fish swung just past me. I managed to grab a stool that was nearby and hit him as hard as I could on his head. I knew that if I had fallen when he hit me, he would have continued to kick me until I died.

At that moment another guard came rushing in and stopped us from further blows. I became frightened, realizing that this would probably not be the end of the problem. I felt certain that after this brawl the clerk had it in for me and would try to find some way to kill me.

The following day when the Komanderfurer from our shift came into the camp, I went up to him and explained what had happened. I told him how the clerk had tried to beat me up and that I had defended myself, hitting him with the stool. The Komanderfurer said, "You should have killed him!"

When I continued explaining that I was afraid the clerk would now be after me, I ended up by asking him to put me on another shift as far away from him as was possible. The Komanderfurer replied, "You are not going. Don't worry." Instead, he immediately went over to the clerk and told him he was being transferred to another location. After that the clerk avoided me, I think he realized that his being taken off the shift had something to do with our encounter.

42

The Puff

Some time during the early months of 1944 the German Officers organized a brothel at Camp Dachau. The brothel was nicknamed the "Puff." Over the previous four years the German Police had already enjoyed the services of unhappy girls who were abducted by the Gestapo and forced into the brothels. German soldiers would often visit the "Puff" to make use of the pleasures provided there.

But later that year, the "Puff" was opened up to everyone when a new rule was issued by the officers in command. The labor camps were sent several prostitutes for their disposal. When the "Puff" was first established on the site of the camp, only prisoners who were of German origin had been permitted to visit and make use of its services. But later during the year, all male prisoners were able to enter the barrack where several young girls were brought from the women's division.

The terrified girls and young women were held there as slaves and supervised by the "old hands" in the camp. These were the prisoners who had criminal records and were given free reign in how they maintained the "Puff." The brothel was situated at a certain distance from the main area of the barracks, but it was very close to the block that was occupied by the priests.

Some of the prisoners and the priests were appalled at the opening of the "Puff," and they later organized a boycott of its use. They began picketing the house of "White Slavery," as the brothel also became known. It was open only in the evening hours, and the prisoners who wanted to see it closed down planted informers to work at the brothel. The informers would report the names of the visitors to the brothel. Sometimes just before the arrival of guests to the "Puff" hundreds of prisoners would gather at the entrance and greet every visitor with boos and catcalls.

Processions of prisoners would follow the prisoners who were seen leaving the house, shouting at them and spitting in their faces. We discovered that the best results were reached when prisoners spread rumors that the S.S. guards would liquidate the prisoners who frequented the "Puff." Prisoners became afraid that if they visited the brothel, they would be taken for special laboratory tests and lead to their demise. The boycott eventually became successful, and only a few men dared to enter. At length the few remaining prisoners who visited became the target of cruel jokes and insulting remarks by the other prisoners.

Finally, the "Puff" was closed down, and the "white slaves" were transferred to another camp.

43

Fate Stepped In

Not long after that, in March of 1945, all the prisoners were called from the barracks into the *appellplatz*. We were informed that they needed to select two hundred prisoners for a transport to another factory. The S.S. Report Fuehrer picked out the men himself, saying, "Go have your lunch. After lunch you will be sent to the other factory." I was one of the prisoners picked out for the transport.

While we ate lunch, we were visited by Lager Elster who was in charge of the entire camp. Lager Elster was a German but one of the older prisoners who was in charge at the camp. He asked who had been selected from the prisoner group for transport. I quickly replied that I was. Lager Elster asked me how long I had been in prisons and which camps I had been in. When I told him about my experience in Camp Stutthof, Lager Elster couldn't believe I had survived. He asked me a lot of questions about Camp Stutthoff and said, "I know what you went through." He gazed at me for a few moments, and then it was clear he had made a decision. "No," he said, "You are not going on that transport."

He told me that when I heard the whistle blow for the transport to leave, I should get under the bed and remain there, and not to come out for any reason. I struggled with my thoughts. I didn't know if I should trust him. I knew very well that if the S.S. guards caught me, I would be shot to death on the spot. But something deep down told me to heed his words. With only the slightest hesitation, I stayed put. When the whistle blew, I got under the bed in the corner and hid there. I did not leave on the transport.

They took everyone else who had been chosen and they marched solemnly from the camp. In a couple of weeks we received word that the transport had gone to a special place. They had been marched to a location not far from the camp. I learned that the group had been stopped abruptly and everyone had been executed and their bodies had been unceremoniously disposed of. As I sat quietly for several moments, I said several prayers for the prisoners whose lives had just ended so horribly. Then I said an additional prayer to God in thankful relief that I had somehow been spared.

44

Prisoners Helping Prisoners

Though everyone was suffering and living in constant terror, we managed to have organized relief as our life in the camp continued. Often an ailing man who was unable to go to work and had been left behind in the camp would receive some extra food that had been gathered by a friend during the day. It might be a raw potato, or a rotten tomato. Sometimes it was only a few cabbage leaves that had been picked up from the ground near the kitchen area. We called it our "organized relief."

We all knew that if our attempt to ease the suffering of our fellow prisoners were discovered, it would mean severe punishment by the S.S. guards. Sometimes the victim would be sent to the gas chamber because he had been helped by others. But the efforts to help each other continued in spite of the fear of discovery. Despite the rampant deterioration of ethics and justice, the inmates of the concentration camps performed many heroic acts of charity. Most of the men in the camps suffered from malnutrition. And that created a beautiful field of action where charity could function.

The healthier men helped the sick and the weak. The stronger prisoners advised and talked with the helpless ones whose spirit was rapidly deteriorating. A famous professor who found himself among the unfortunate prisoners had to be taught how to use a shovel so he could survive. People who had lived in the cities had to learn from their comrades how to till the soil and work with their hands.

A newcomer soon signed his own death warrant if his neighbors and fellow prisoners failed to acquaint him with the rules of the camp. He usually had difficulty believing that he would not be allowed to rest for a few minutes during a strenuous assignment. But when he attracted the negative attention of the S.S. guards, both he and his companions would suffer equally from the cruel reprisals and tortures. If a prisoner tried to sit down to rest, the other prisoners would be on the lookout and urge him to continue in spite of his inability to continue.

At the camp everyone had to wait for their piece of bread, for their coffee, or for their bowl of warm soup. There were lines to wait for the meager food, there were lines in front of the communal bath, and there were lines in front of the latrine. Prisoners had to live and die with the lines becoming a fact of life. Even in the lines, though, charity could be found. The younger and stronger men would give their places to the aged and the infirm. They would often try to cheer one another up with jokes or simple words of encouragement.

Nowhere else can the power of the encourage word become as great and potent as in a death camp. Words by the guards would crush out the will to live, and the right words from a friend or a fellow comrade would heal our wounds and sometimes bring relief. Even words crept into the camps and made their way to each one of us, but it was the good words that helped to repair the damage and restore our faith in mankind. A kind word proved in many cases to be more valuable than a loaf of bread.

When fellow prisoners were very despondent and feeling hopeless, it was sufficient to bring them some good news, even if the news had been invented. When I heard rumors that the situation on the fronts was "improving," which meant the impending doom of Hitler's armies, I appreciated that word more than a piece of bread and butter.

News that was positive helped many prisoners pull through their worst hours.

45

Feelings and Thoughts about the Death Camp

The prisoners would sometimes talk about their feelings about the camp and how their lives had changed drastically. When we entered Concentration Camp Dachau and the other camps, the gates had the words, "Arbeit Macht Frei" imprinted in huge letters. The words were in German, and they meant "Hard work makes you free." The slogan was placed there at the entrance as a reminder that there was no exit from the camp other than through the crematorium chimney. Only death could set you free.

A death camp is a place where the natural order is constantly violated. It was never a question of whether we would live or die, but merely a question of time: When we would die. No one escaped. The prisoners knew that there was no way out.

Prisoners were divided by sex and their general physical condition. The strong prisoners were forced to work. The weak prisoners were systematically murdered. When we talked together, we often talked about our "journey's end" through death. Death became our constant companion and we never knew when it would be our turn to leave this world. Because of this threat and daily fear, many of the men began to lose their faith that we would be saved. You could actually see some of the men lose their will and motivation to survive.

As time went on, everyone became hardened to the reality of our condition. Natural and violent deaths would fail to stir us. We had seen too many bloody spectacles when the S.S. guards would slaughter innocent victims without mercy. We no longer felt frustration rage within us when we saw a comrade or fellow prisoner killed without provocation, realizing there was nothing we could do to help or comfort the victim.

We became accustomed to the sight of corpses. We slept among them and walked over them. We became only half alive. The living almost looked like corpses as well, the bones showed through from the weight loss that everyone experienced. We knew that for German executioners to kill a man was as unimportant to them as crushing a mosquito. We also knew that to approach a dying person would bring on a dreadful punishment. The person who wanted to offer help and comfort would be kicked and clubbed for his efforts.

46

Camp Dachau Was Changing

My life at Camp Dachau continued to be lived in constant fear, frustration, and terror. Every day the bombings would go on around us, and there were many rumors going around about the German captors. The prisoners didn't know what to believe, if there was indeed an end in sight. But I was soon to learn that fate would play another hand. There was to be yet another turn of events in store for me.

In the early part of April in 1945 our work load had been cut down to just one shift. The S.S. Officials didn't want to have too many prisoners sitting around idle. Plans were made to send my shift to another factory near Berlin for job detail. This was one of the factories that were having work done on the bombs.

This time there were about a thousand prisoners being transferred by cattle boxcars. When the boxcars had traveled about halfway to Berlin, they abruptly came to a stop because the railroad had been bombed. They kept us in the closed boxcars for more than eight hours. There was no food or water and everyone was in a state of panic. I became very frightened that we would all be killed immediately.

Not long afterwards, there came another order to bring us all back to Camp Dachau. While we were being transported back to camp, I caught a glimpse of the many bombed-out areas. There were railroads that had been ripped apart, stations that no longer looked like their original structures, and bridges that could no longer be used along the way. Countryside that had once been beautiful and unspoiled now looked like a disaster area. It was unbelievable that the bombings could have caused so much destruction and devastation. We finally arrived back at Camp Dachau on April 3, 1945.

The camp was now in utter chaos because everyone had an eerie feeling that the end was not far in the distant future. The guards placed me in Barrack No. 16, and assigned me to work in a group that was digging anti-tank ditches. When my group went out on work detail, the capos and S.S. Guards would beat us with a renewed fury, clubbing the prisoners at every opportunity. We would hear shouts to work faster, and anyone who became weak or sick was thrown onto a big trailer. Once they were placed on that trailer, everyone knew it meant being taken to the gas chamber and then to be cremated.

When I was near my barrack after one of those work details, I met one of the priests I had gotten to know who was living in a nearby barrack. He asked me how I was doing and I replied, "It's really bad, Father. I don't think I will make it." I told him that working out in the ditches was terrible and that the guards were whipping people to death for no reason.

The priest then came up with an idea that I believe ultimately saved my life. He urged me to join the group of priests when they were in the courtyard for appell. He said to wait until I heard the whistle to form our work groups. Then I should quickly join their group, trying not to call too much attention to myself.

This stroke of luck proved to be a turning point for me. For the next two weeks I managed to avoid going out on work detail with the other prisoners. Catholic priests, who totaled over two thousand, were being treated more leniently when it was rumored that the Pope in Rome had blessed the German soldiers. The priests were retained as a group in a certain area where they needed a password to enter and exit.

After I was given advice from the priest, I managed to join their group and went back with them to their barrack. There the priests had tables arranged, and they were working on simple tasks like repairing tents. And it was there that I remained, working with them until it was time to return to the main camp area for dinner. Each day I managed to return to my own barrack after having learned the secret password that needed to be uttered when stopped by a guard. I managed to remain safe for about two weeks, returning to my barrack only for meals or to sleep.

But then an order was received at the camp from the Reichsfuehrer, S.S. Heinrich Himmler, that handing the camp over was out of the question. The camp would have to be evacuated. The order stated that no prisoners were to fall into the hands of the enemy alive. Many of the prisoners had no idea what the Nazis intended. But the tension in the camp was very high and we all knew that trouble was in the air.

At about ten minutes before midnight on April 9th, everyone was awakened brusquely and ordered to line up outside the barracks. S.S. Guards and other members of the prisoner police force searched the buildings thoroughly, even slashing the mattresses as they passed through. After about ninety minutes, the prisoners were permitted to return to sleep: The inspection was over for now. All the prisoners, me included, were pale and very nervous. We didn't expect to survive the night.

I learned that the day before, the commandant and his staff had worried about the possibility of concealed knives and firearms in the prison compound. They were afraid of a prisoner insurrection. Knowing that their control of the prisoners was getting out of hand, plans were quickly made to massacre everyone. At the designated time, the barracks were surrounded by S.S. troopers with their machine guns ready. The action was verbally squelched by the S.S. camp surgeon who didn't agree with the planned massacre, he thought there had been too much death already and that there should be no more killing. The commandant in charge of the camp then decided to search the barracks again for weapons. He needed justification for the executions and he planned that if weapons were found, it would be the proof he needed. Luckily for us, nothing was found, and I was thankful that we had received a reprieve from death.

On the 24th of April, 1945, an S.S. order was received that all valuables and remaining food should be loaded onto trucks. For the last two days even before the order came, the German guards must have realized that the American troops were getting closer; we noticed that they were taking food on trucks away from the camp. They had begun feeding us only every second day. Our meal became a scant portion of soup and a much smaller piece of bread. They even stopped taking the prisoners out on work detail. Prisoners were walking around constantly hungry and frightened. We all had the feeling that something was about to happen.

The circumstances were very ominous, and we worried that we would soon be on the move again. But the order that arrived could not be implemented because the presence of American planes discouraged any highway traffic. We were unable to sleep under these conditions. For what seemed an eternity we were kept huddled in the rooms.

There were other rumors that the S.S. intended to move everyone out of the camp that very afternoon and evening. But again the American planes put a stop to that. American fighter planes constantly swept over the camp area, and the prisoners would wave at them when they saw them. The areas around the camp and the railroad station were being bombed constantly. This brought great joy to the prisoners.

47

The Last Days of Dachau

As we approached the end of our imprisonment, every hour that passed was a sweet victory over death. The prisoners did not foresee that most Nazi attempts to evacuate the camp would fail because daylight travel was almost impossible. Convoys and trains were constantly being bombed by American fighter planes. Many times toward the end, prisoners were called out of their barracks to form columns and go out on a death march. But the death march would often be disrupted by the onslaught of fighter planes that would suddenly appear in the area.

There was constant confusion everywhere. I had always wanted to survive, and it had been my frequent hope that I would manage to stay alive. But I knew, too, that my chances of dying were still great. Now, with the possibility of liberation close at hand, in a few weeks or even days away, it became important to stay alive.

The chaos continued and reached even greater proportions. We lived in peril believing that our lives were in greater jeopardy than before. We had endured years of cruel confinement. We believed we were doomed. We couldn't believe that the victorious American troops would reach the camp in time to prevent our slaughter by the hated S.S. guards.

In our minds we dreadfully foresaw the moment when the prisoner police would whip us into line and we would be marched by S.S. Troopers through the gate. We could visualize them marching us to a gloomy Bavarian forest where they would riddle our bodies with machine gun bullets. Everyone knew the German leaders wanted no witnesses left alive of their atrocities.

The Germans formed a camp police that was made up of prisoners to control other prisoners. Our hunger became much worse as food was in very short supply. I had to skip many meals because there wasn't any food. Prisoners were not able to work during those last few days. I walked into the room where I slept and noticed another prisoner who had recently been made a "prisoner police." I asked him why he didn't bring us some food because we hadn't had anything to eat in a while. The prisoner replied that he was disgusted with everything, the entire situation. He told me to use his arm band if I wanted to and go out to try to find food. I agreed.

I placed his armband on my left arm and headed toward the kitchen. Quietly I entered the kitchen trying to think how I could find food. I didn't know how to ask for food, but I remembered that I had recently heard that one of the cooks was from Warsaw and had my aunt's maiden name. I wondered if he could possibly be related to me. As I approached the first cook I came across, an idea came to me. First I explained our dire plight and how we were suffering from a lack of food. Then I asked about the cook I had heard about, that perhaps he was at the camp and maybe I could speak with him.

The cook I was speaking with called the head cook over, and to my surprise, he turned out to be a distant relative of my family, a cousin. He hugged me tightly and confirmed that he knew me and my family. He expressed surprise to find me at this camp. He then suggested that arrangements be made for me to work in the kitchen with him. He quickly gave me some food that I was able to take back to the barrack with me for the other prisoners.

Using a paper requisition he gave me, I went to the camp office for an immediate transfer to work in the kitchen. They were surprised in the office since they felt we were close to the end of the war. But nevertheless, they made the necessary arrangements. When I returned to my barrack and gave the prisoner guard back his armband, he was shocked that I had not only gotten us food, but I was now assigned to be a cook in the kitchen.

The next day I learned that while I had been reporting to the kitchen area for my new assignment, German guards had come to our barrack and taken the entire group of prisoners on a death march. They had been taken through a forest to an unknown location. I felt heartsick to learn that all the prisoners had been machine gunned and that there had been no survivors. I felt that I had gotten to know many of the men as we had shared the common goal of trying to survive.

The prisoners who were still in the camp were ushered together in a separate barrack. Food supplies at the camp continued to dwindle even further. Many of the prisoners that remained were repulsed by the odor of the food that was rationed out. The soups resembled dirty water. The number of prisoner deaths continued to rise, yet we still had hope that the end was somehow near. April 26th brought still more disorder. At about 9 o'clock in the morning an order was read aloud that the camp was to be evacuated. Prisoners were to assemble at roll call, carrying their meager possessions.

But an underground committee had already been formed in Camp Dachau. They did everything in their power to create havoc and sabotage the S.S. plans. All of the records of the prisoners that were being kept in the camp labor office were quickly burned. The guards became concerned only with their own future because they realized the end was near.

During the night, I heard the thunder of heavy artillery, and I was literally counting the hours between myself and Victory Day. Suddenly the news of a transfer to a camp in Tyrol in Austria spread like wildfire. A few prisoners became hysterical at the thought of yet another excruciating experience. But a few hours later, we learned the truth. Our blocks were promptly cleared. Prisoners were ordered to gather in the yard and be ready to depart for an unknown destination. Prisoners were milling about wildly, but thousands of them obeyed the orders. The guards assembled about seven thousand prisoners from some of the other barracks to be taken from the camp.

Those of us who remained in the camp watched as the prisoners were divided into huge groups to be marched from the area. Small amounts of food were passed out to them before they left at 10 o'clock that night. We learned later that after about twenty kilometers from Munich, in a forest, they had been machine gunned in groups. But the guards had been somewhat careless in their massacre, and about sixty of the prisoners managed to survive to tell of their experience.

On the morning of April 27th, a group of prisoners was being prepared for another march to their death when there was a commotion on the grounds. The distraction was caused by a transport that was arriving from Concentration Camp Buchenwald. The column of marching prisoners looked like skeletons as they entered the main gate. We watched in horror as they stumbled and slowly walked into the compound. There were about two thousand and five hundred men, and I felt as if I was seeing a nightmare come to life. Many of them were barefoot and their feet were bleeding. They had very little clothing on their bodies.

Six hundred of them were taken to the camp hospital immediately. Two hundred of them never reached the hospital: They died that afternoon on the camp grounds. According to one account that was related to me later, each prisoner had been given a loaf of bread, and that had been their only food for the two-week period it had taken them to reach Camp Dachau. Many of the prisoner bodies were scattered all over the grounds and then later stacked in the crematorium. Some of the remaining Dachau prisoners believed that they had been saved from imminent death by the Buchenwald survivors who managed to distract the S.S. men and prisoner police, giving them the ten precious hours.

Late that evening, we watched as a group of prisoners that

consisted of men, women, and children, were quickly hurried through the camp and out of the gate by a heavily-armed escort. We didn't know who they were or why they were being taken from the camp. To this day I still wonder who those people had been and why they were secretly ushered away just before Liberation Day.

All the other prisoners remained in Camp Dachau until the very end. There was a feeling of apprehension as we wondered what would happen next. A feeling of tension was heavy in the air and you could feel the fear that was overwhelming. The people in charge were too panicky to handle the tense situation. There were only a small number of guards visible in the area, and they had trouble keeping order.

On the 28th of April, 1945, the battle front was only about ten kilometers away. The nearer the battle came, the fewer the number of Nazi S.S. guards remaining in the camp became. Only about one hundred guards remained. Most of the officers were gone; they had run away in anticipation of the arrival of the armed forces. Members of the prisoners' committee moved out into the open, and there was a rumor going around that it was important to refrain from any contact with the S.S. guards. Some of the guards had been helpful during the last few months, they were aware of the progress of the allies.

There were additional rumors that the Camp Commandant had summoned four old-time prisoners, one of whom was a priest, to his office. After about two hours, they had emerged from the office with smiles on their faces. It was believed that he had given up his command and that he had introduced them to an official of the International Red Cross.

48

Liberation Day

Freedom finally arrived on a Sunday. It was the 29th of April, 1945. This was the day that approximately 32,000 people of 31 different nationalities were liberated. Yes! Freedom at Last! It was a day that will forever be burned in my memory. When it finally came, prisoners looked stunned that it was a reality and it took a while to comprehend the major event.

The stage had actually been set about two weeks earlier with Heinrich Himmler. Himmler was the head of Hitler's S.S. security forces, and he had sent a telegram to Camp Dachau stating that surrender of the camp to the enemy was not in the plan. The following week he had followed up with another telegram instructing the officials to massacre the entire camp population. That massacre was scheduled for Sunday, April 29, 1945 at 8 p.m. in the evening.

On that fateful Sunday, I was working in the camp kitchen at around 5 o'clock in the afternoon. After work I walked back to the barracks as was my usual routine. Just as I began crossing the courtyard that led to the barracks, I heard what sounded like gunfire from a nearby post. With a sudden realization that it was someone shooting, I jumped and could feel a bullet whiz by my head. Without much forethought, I dropped to the ground as if I had been shot. I lay there for several minutes, trying to understand what was happening.

Fearing that the guards were starting to finish everyone off, I jumped to my feet and ran quickly behind the barrack, trying to find a hiding place. It took a few minutes to catch my breath and try to gather my thoughts. Uncertain as to where the best place would be, I decided to run to my own barrack. I was certain that the guards had already started killing the prisoners.

As I rushed inside, I slowed my pace a little because I saw the other prisoners just going on about their business as if nothing had happened. I looked around at my fellow prisoners, not sure if I should alarm them and cause a panic. Just as I looked about for a safe place to sit down, I suddenly heard shouts outside of "Americans! Americans!"

Scores of remaining prisoners filled the courtyard in a matter of minutes. Some of the prisoners ran toward the barbed-wire fence, shouting "Americans" as they ran. As I ran toward the fence I could see two American soldiers walking up to the main gate, but the gate was closed. There was a side door that led into the gate office, so I approached that room cautiously with a few of the other prisoners. We ran up the stairway that led to the main office area, and we found it had been deserted.

We looked out the window and realized that it was too high to jump down to the ground without injury. I grabbed some long drapes that were hanging by the windows and ripped them into long strips. I urged the other prisoners to help me tie them into a long rope. With as much speed as I could muster, I tied one end of our make-shift rope to the steam radiator and tossed the other end out the window so we could slide down the outside of the building.

We worked together to climb down that rope to reach the ground below. I rushed to the gate area that had been pulled open and came upon a jeep with two American G.I.'s entering the camp and jumped inside their jeep with very little urging. They had machine guns in their hands as we drove around the camp to clean the guard posts. They drove to the end of the camp, and then slowly turned around to return to the main gate.

On the drive back to the front of the camp, I talked with the soldiers, explaining that I was an American who had been imprisoned in the camp. Quickly I told them about my circumstances and how I had somehow managed to stay alive. During our conversation, I mentioned that I had worked in the camp kitchen toward the end. They were astonished that I had survived.

Thousands of prisoners shuffled out into the courtyard, looking dazed and confused. Nearby, many bodies of the dead lay on the ground. It was a sight upon which the American soldiers looked on in disbelief. The prisoners were skeletal beings who looked severely undernourished. Faces were filthy and the odor of not having been washed in a long time filled the air.

We discovered that some of the other prisoners had rounded up the S.S. guards in one of the watchtowers, grabbed their guns, and then shot them with their own weapons. The guards in the second tower held out a white flag of surrender. But when the American soldiers came up to them, the guards opened fire shooting randomly. They were quickly subdued by the American soldiers and taken into confinement.

Many sick and dying men crawled on their hands and knees, some of them were without clothing and others were covered only with rags. They leaned on walls or were supported by their stronger comrades. It was a sad procession of staggering, frightening skeletons that made its way through the crowd. Some of them found enough energy to walk as far as the fence.

The jeep I was in reached the main gate, and I was happy to have the soldiers as my escort. The commanding officers asked who I was, and the soldiers explained that I was an American who had been falsely put into the camps. They also related my comment that I had worked in the camp kitchen. I was stunned when the General came up to me, shook my hand, and said that I would be in charge of the kitchen.

Just a short time later, another officer appeared at the main entrance and there was a flurry of activity that was exciting to see. There was a group of prisoners standing nearby. They had rushed over because they wanted to meet the soldiers who had liberated them. It was a memorable occasion as the ex-prisoners were able to shake the hands of the soldiers, and there was a lot of hugging and hand-shaking going on.

The Dachau Commandant Haupstumfuehrer Weiss had been caught and brought into the camp. He was later taken out onto the balcony to face the surviving prisoners. And it was discovered that several of the S.S. guards had somehow mysteriously disappeared, but they were found later wearing civilian clothes. Some of them had tried to hide in prisoner clothing, they were wearing the striped pajama-like clothes we had worn while we had been imprisoned there.

As the first night of freedom arrived, there were still rumors flourishing that many of the S.S. soldiers had managed to survive and that they would return to attack the camp that night. The fear that they would retake it and massacre everyone was unlikely, yet it caused some restless moments. Fear was in the air, and everyone had trouble believing that freedom had finally arrived. As I lay down to sleep that night, I breathed a sigh of relief that this day had finally come! I could actually feel the taste of freedom as I realized it was real.

The American soldiers who had liberated Camp Dachau were shocked at the crowd of men before them. Many of the soldiers were very young and had never experienced such a sight. They exclaimed that it was like looking at skeletons that were alive and moving about. I could see tears in the eyes of some of the soldiers as they looked at the terrible sight that was everywhere in the camp.

The soldiers began working frantically to try to alleviate the despair and plight of the people who were desperately in need of nourishment in order to survive. They brought out food from the camp warehouses so the liberated prisoners could eat. The entire stock of canned food vanished in no time.

A few hours later, the American soldiers were surprised when they had to take care of hundreds of victims who were suffering from deadly and severe cramps. The stomachs of the severely weakened men had become unable to digest the huge amount of food that had been available. After a lengthy starvation diet of several years, one square meal had suddenly become a deadly poison.

Chaos still was running rampant in the area. I had been put in total charge of the camp kitchen, and I set about the task of organizing the crew they had provided me. It was a struggle to prepare the gigantic meals that were needed for everyone at the camp. On one occasion, I remember being interviewed by a reporter who was visiting the camp. He was astonished that I was an American. He expressed amazement that I was both an American and a Catholic who had somehow managed to survive the horror of the camps.

The following day, an American captain and sergeant came into the camp specifically looking for me. When they couldn't locate me, they left a message that I would be contacted in a day or two. It was on May 2, 1945, that the sergeant again returned in a jeep and escorted me to the headquarters to meet with Colonel Clyde Joyce. Colonel Joyce explained that he had learned from outside sources that I had been in the camp with another American. We had many conferences at their headquarters and discussed the transfer of several people from Camp Dachau to a place called Freimann near Munich, "The S.S. Kaserne."

At that point it was decided that the camp would be used to imprison the S.S. guards who had been captured. They divided the Appellplatz into sections with a barbed-wire fence creating the perimeters. Just outside the camp area, they erected bleachers. Once a week they held a show to display the imprisoned S.S. men to the public. The ex-prisoners who had been held captive by the S.S. guards and officials were able to sit in those bleachers while the S.S. men were paraded in a line, single file, in front of them.

If a guard was recognized by one of the ex-prisoners as having beaten or killed people, he was pointed out to the American soldiers and a mark was then placed on him. At the same time, if someone was recognized as having helped the ex-prisoners, he was then placed in a special group, a group that was treated more leniently.

This was the camp atmosphere that I continued to live in until the autumn of 1945. They kept me in charge of the kitchen and mess hall for the entire camp, complimenting me on the fine job I was doing. I was responsible for the feeding of the many ex-prisoners and civilians who arrived frequently to act as witnesses during the wartime trials at Dachau. I also worked with the military personnel, serving as an interpreter at the American headquarters.

49

Home Again

Finally, in August of 1945, I had an interview with the American intelligence officers at their office in the city of Dachau. They suggested that I return back to my family in Poland to begin my life again and try to pick up the pieces. It was believed that this would be an easier task because my papers were already in order. They thanked me for my work in supervising the kitchen and said that I had been a real asset to them. Thus began my preparations to return home over the next few months.

Before traveling to my own village in Poland, though, I went first to Kudowa Zdroj, another town in Poland. There I registered again at the American Embassy in October of 1945. When the embassy officials realized that I had been in the concentration death camps, especially Dachau and Stutthof, they were amazed. They actually closed the entire embassy for the day as if it were a holiday.

Everyone who worked at the embassy came into the room to visit with me because they wanted to hear about my experiences. I had also brought along many pictures from the concentration camps, showing the horror and terrible conditions that had been endured by the prisoners. They were taken by the U. S. soldiers who liberated us, and they gave me a copy because of the horrors I had lived through. Some of those pictures can be seen on the following pages, I still have them in my memory album as a reminder of my life in the Camps. Everyone asked questions about my imprisonment as an American. They were astonished that I had managed to survive the horror of several camps and for so many years.

The American consul was impressed and looked at me with wonder in his eyes. He couldn't believe that I had managed to survive the death camps. He shook his head in disbelief, and then he hugged me in farewell as I prepared to leave for my home. His parting words stood out in my memory: He made a vow then and there that he would see to it himself that I would be the first person to leave Poland on the very first U.S. ship that arrived.

"You endured so much at the hands of your captors," he said. "I can imagine all that you went through, it must have been terrible!" As he shook my hand again, he said it was the least they could do for me. After that memorable visit, I continued my journey back to my family home.

***

This was the entrance to Camp Dachau. The gate had the words "Arbeit Macht Frei," which was German for "Work Makes You Free."

The ex-prisoners looked on as their captors were held captive for their atrocities.

This barbed wire fence comprised the walls in our compound that were a constant reminder of our captivity.

This was the compound at Camp Dachau, with the barrack visible on the right.

These photographs show the ex-prisoners walking about
the grounds of Camp Dachau after liberation.

This photograph shows the soldiers in the Camp,
talking with the newly-liberated prisoners.

U.S. Soldiers walked about the buildings at the Camp,
as the liberated prisoners experienced freedom at last.

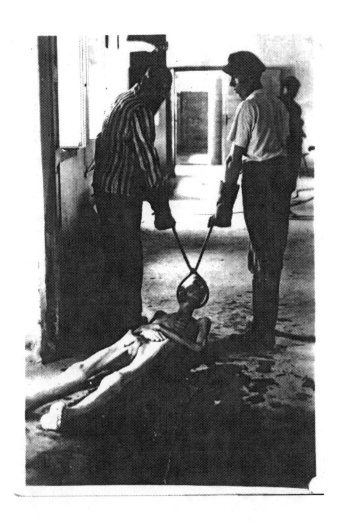

This photograph shows bodies being transported
to their final resting place.

The pile of bodies shows the horror and devastation
that greeted the U.S. soldiers who liberated us.

Bodies thrown together were a final reminder of the horrors and death was the fate of thousands of people at the Camp.

This photograph shows the terrible sight of human remains that greeted the young U.S. soldiers who liberated us from the Death Camp.

This photograph shows the soldiers just after liberation,
looking around the Camp at the terrible conditions
that had become our daily lives.

This photograph is the sight that greeted the soldiers
as they walked about the camp, a visual reminder
of the executions that took place.

These pictures show the trains used to eliminate prisoners.
This was how they placed them in boxcars to die.
They were known as the "Box Car Executions."

Additional pictures of the "Box Car Executions."

The memory of bodies lying around,
waiting to be removed is forever buried in my mind.

This was an example of the tortures inflicted on the prisoners.

***

My family was overjoyed to see me when I returned to my village in Poland. When I walked in the door, there was a moment of silence as they gazed at me with shock. They had been afraid that I had been killed and they would never see me again. One by one, they rushed up and hugged me, crying at my haggard appearance. I was a thin resemblance of the person I had been before my camp experience. But the joy they felt was clear on their faces as I embraced them once again.

My parents had been preparing to attend a wedding celebration, and my entrance was taken in stride as they grabbed me by the arm and pulled me out the door. "Come with us," they said.

"But I'm not dressed for a wedding," I protested. "What would the people think?"

"Nonsense," said my mother. "Everyone will be overjoyed to see you and visit with you."

When we arrived at the wedding, people gathered around me to hear about my experiences. Friends and my family kept a steady pace of questions that seemed to be unending.

After that it didn't take long for news of my return to spread. When we returned home after the wedding, neighbors rushed over to celebrate my return. My friends from the area came over, too, and there were lots of hugs and claps on my back. Everyone wanted to hear about my experiences: they wanted to hear what the concentration camps had been like, and there were many questions about the terrible ordeal I had lived through. The underlying feeling was one of shock and disbelief that I had managed to return alive to rejoin my family.

I started courting Jean, the young neighbor girl I had met before the war. I learned more about her and her family as my wounds were starting to heal. She was also an American. Her father had been a supervisor in the company that was building the Empire State Building. Sometime during the 1930s their family had taken a tour to Poland, and it was at that time that her father had become paralyzed in his legs. Her younger brother had also been arrested by the Gestapo back in 1941. In fact, he was the youngest of all the American internees who were in the two internment camps, Laufen and Titomonic. Her brother had managed to survive the war and had ventured to Michigan to begin a new life.

Our courtship was brief, and it wasn't long before we were making plans to spend our future together. We wanted to get married as soon as possible, so we went to visit the Catholic parish priest. But problems arose when he informed me that because we were both Americans we couldn't get married without special permission. So I went to see the Bishop and asked for special permission for the marriage to take place. He conferred with his aides and finally gave me a letter to the parish priest allowing the marriage.

Once the wedding ceremony had taken place, the priest informed me that there was another snag. Because we were both Americans, we would have to be married in a civil service office as well. A week later Jean and I visited a civil service office, but they told us we needed permission from the U.S. embassy in Warsaw. I couldn't believe the amount of red-tape I kept running into just to be able to start my life on the right path.

It was our plan to return to America and begin our life together in the country where we had both been born. Both Jean and I prepared to journey to America, but we discovered that it was not a simple task to leave Poland even if you were American.

Needless to say, there was a great deal of running around, but we finally ended up at the embassy in Warsaw. As I waited in line to see the secretary at the embassy, I discovered that some people had already been sent to America after the war. I was very surprised since I had been told that I would be among the first people sent back to the United States by the consul back in October. I remembered the words of the Consul vividly and felt betrayed.

When my turn finally came to see the secretary, I asked her why I hadn't been sent back to the United States as promised. She answered, "You were just unlucky. We skipped October, November, and December of 1945 and started sending people from January of

1946." She added, then, that they were also taking care of people who had been arrested, jailed, or persecuted as Americans. I quickly informed her that I had been one of those people.

She looked at me dumbfounded, as if she couldn't believe what she was hearing. She immediately called in the U.S. Consul. As soon as he walked into the room, he recognized me at once. Realizing what had transpired, he apologized for not taking care of me sooner and promised that I would be on the next available ship that arrived.

The problem of my marriage to another American came up then, and the consul said there should be no problem; he gave me the necessary permission to get married in Poland, along with a letter authorizing both of us for travel. From that point on things seemed to go smoother for us. We waited impatiently for news that the next ship was to arrive.

While we waited, I tried to join groups of Polish survivors of the concentration camps. I was hoping that meeting with other people who had suffered what I had suffered would help me begin a healing process. I was saddened to discover that the Polish prisoners I had come to know while in the camps didn't want to associate with me after the war. They said that I was an American, and that I should look for groups of survivors who were also American. I couldn't believe it! Men who I thought were my friends and comrades now turned away from me. I suffered in silence as the mental images of the camps came flooding to the surface without warning.

The wait took several months of additional waiting, months that brought even more change into our lives. My wife Jean had become pregnant within months of our marriage, and we had another member added to our family. Our daughter was born in January, and we named her Danuta. The happy event brought us joy, but it also created a new problem. We received notification that we were to leave on a ship for America, the Ernie Pyle, but we didn't have the necessary papers for our daughter to travel with us.

When we managed to get a hold of the U.S. Consul, he said that it would not be a problem. "Because it's you, I will make sure that all three of you will travel together. Take your daughter with you," he said. "Even though she doesn't have her travel documents yet, I will personally come to the port to carry your daughter on board the ship and guarantee her passage to America." He still planned to try to get the papers our daughter needed in time, though we only had one week before our scheduled sailing.

Jean and I worried that something would go wrong, and we would not be able to make the journey. We waited with eager anticipation for the big day to arrive. That morning we left our home in Poland and hugged our family goodbye as we left. I said a little prayer to God before we left for the ship, asking him to watch over my family in Poland and take care of us on our journey to our new life. Ultimately, the problem of traveling with our daughter was solved when we arrived at the port and prepared to board the ship. The Consul had arrived to greet us, and he planned to carry Danuta on board the ship himself. His importance as the American Consul meant that no one would question our daughter's passage on the ship. But just as we started to board with the Consul carrying the baby, a courier arrived with the necessary papers, and we were able to leave without further trouble.

The trip took just over a week, and Jean nursed and took care of our baby. Traveling with an infant was difficult, but the realization that we would soon be on American soil again kept our hopes high. It was a beautiful sight to finally see the Statue of Liberty in the horizon as our ship neared our destination.

50

Arrival in America

We arrived in New York in the winter of 1948, with our baby daughter, Danuta, and just our suitcases to start a new life together. We showed our daughter's name as the American pronunciation of her name, Diane, on her papers. For a short time we stayed with my wife's cousin in New York, but we soon felt the urge to set up our home in Michigan so we could begin anew.

We journeyed to Hamtramck where we found a very simple place to live, renting a room from another family. It was a small room that we quickly outgrew, but it was a beginning. I found work immediately because it was a real necessity for our survival. We had no money and needed everything. As time went on, we were able to buy a home in Hamtramck and slowly improved our way of living; but it was a real struggle for the first few years. My wife's brother, Eddie, came to live with us for a while until he was able to make a life for himself.

In August of 1951 another major change occurred in our lives. My wife gave birth to a second addition to our family. With the birth of our son, Dennis, our family life continued to improve. In spite of the long hours I had to work to provide for my family, we were happy. Life was certainly different for me in America. I had a family, a home, and a job. The future looked good.

Yet the memories of those horrible years in the concentration camps would come often in the beginning. For the first few years I would frequently wake up in a cold sweat, trembling from the nightmares of the tortures and horrors of the camps. Sometimes I would wake up in the middle of the night screaming in terror as I remembered the occasions when I had almost met my death. My wife would try to comfort me, but it would always take a while for the reality of my new life to sink in.

My work for an automobile manufacturer caused me to travel a long distance from our home in Hamtramck to Willow Run in Ypsilanti. This was in the 1950s, and we didn't have the expressways that are available today. So eventually we began to search for a home out in the suburbs. We had a home built in the suburbs of Detroit, and it was thrilling to watch it going up on the empty lot we had selected. When at last we were able to move in, we packed up our belongings and made the move happily.

Our lives had changed dramatically for the better, but the memories of the German concentration death camps still come back to haunt me. They are forever burned into my mind. I'll be eating a holiday meal, and there will be a flash of a mental image of a meal I had been eating in the camps. It would be fleeting, but it was a reminder of the past.

The stories I have told are unbelievable and shocking. There are thousands of other prisoners who also survived the horror to tell their unbelievable stories. What is important to remember is that these are all true stories told by people, like myself, who were there. We witnessed with our own eyes the atrocities that were committed against anyone the S.S. Guards didn't like. They actually enjoyed punishing a prisoner for the smallest infraction. And they tried not to leave any eyewitnesses alive to tell the world. The victims of the death camps were murdered in cold blood.

Yes, the memories won't go away. It was a long time before I was able to stop the nightmares from coming daily. As time went on, the nightmares would occur less frequently, but they still came. Even now, later in life, I have constant reminders of my horrifying experiences. I suffer from headaches and mental anguish whenever I think about the past.

I tried to find some comfort and consolation by sharing my memories with other survivors of the concentration camps. But the groups I tried to communicate with in the area actually turned me away because I was not a Jew. They said that I should look for a group that was especially for Catholics. I was shocked by their callousness! I believed we had all suffered the tortures and near-death experiences. In the camps I had worked side-by-side with people of all nationalities and faiths. I couldn't believe that I was being discriminated against here in America!

Remembrance of the people who died in those camps is forever etched in my memory. I have come to realize that life in the camps was very fragile. Not a day goes by that I don't think about the other prisoners who died or those who had lost hope of ever getting out alive and returning to life as they had known it before. Yes, life does go on, but you don't forget.

51

Journey's End

My father was a survivor. He was a strong man who made a life in America for himself and his family. I watched him struggle with the memories of the physical and mental tortures he had suffered through. My love of reading came from him. He learned a great deal from reading. I would watch him read every newspaper he came in contact with. He would sit religiously with scissors in hand and cut out articles that he found interesting or that he might want to read again later. It would become a family joke when we would pick up a newspaper section to read, only to discover gaping holes in the pages because articles had been taken out.

He kept folders on every subject and always could find the information he wanted to share with us easily from those folders. He would take pains to write the date carefully at the top of each article to keep the information up-to-date. Learning as much as he could about all kinds of information became a hobby for him. Often he would visit the library and read books about different subjects just because he found them interesting. My brother and I were both encouraged to pursue our education after high school by his example. Learning became a very important part of our lives as it had become an intricate part of his life.

And he told us about his life and his family. My brother and I would sit and listen to him for hours as he told us about his experiences in the death camps. He would tell us the stories of the people he had met in the concentration camps who had suffered as he had. He told us about saying prayers for the dead prisoners who would never return to their families. I wrote reports and papers in school about his experiences at every opportunity, and my teachers would read my papers about his life and how he had survived the camps with fascination.

Yes, it was sad to see the torture in his eyes as he talked about his life and the years that had been taken away from him. It was almost impossible to imagine how he had managed so many narrow escapes with death. There must have been a guardian angel that watched over him and helped him escape death so many times. My most vivid memory is of seeing his eyes fill with tears as he told us about watching other men die and not being able to help them.

This was his story.

Printed in the United States
108790LV00002B/304-306/A